ORGANIZATIONAL TROUBLESHOOTING

ORGANIZATIONAL TROUBLESHOOTING

Asking the Right Questions,
Finding the Right Answers

Reed E. Nelson

QUORUM BOOKS
Westport, Connecticut • London

Library of Congress Cataloging-in-Publication Data

658.022
N42o

Nelson, Reed E. (Reed Elliot)
    Organizational troubleshooting : asking the right questions,
finding the right answers / Reed E. Nelson.
        p.   cm.
    Includes bibliographical references and index.
    ISBN 1–56720–046–X (alk. paper)
        1. Small business—Management.   2. Organization.   3. Social
networks.   4. Industrial management—Decision making.   I. Title.
HD62.7.N45   1997
658.02′2—dc20   95–51414

British Library Cataloguing in Publication Data is available.

Library of Congress Catalog Card Number: 95–51414
ISBN: 1–56720–046–X

First published in 1997

Quorum Books, 88 Post Road West, Westport, CT 06881
An imprint of Greenwood Publishing Group, Inc.

Printed in the United States of America

The paper used in this book complies with the
Permanent Paper Standard issued by the National
Information Standards Organization (Z39.48–1984).

10 9 8 7 6 5 4 3 2 1

Copyright Acknowledgments

The author and publisher gratefully acknowledge permission to use the following:

Excerpts from Reed E. Nelson and K. Michael Mathews, "The Use of Cause Maps and Social Net-
work Analysis in Organizational Diagnosis," *Journal of Applied Behavioral Science, 27*: 379–397.
Copyright © 1991 by Reed E. Nelson and K. Michael Mathews. Reprinted by permission of Sage
Publications, Inc.

Excerpts from Paul Hawken, *Growing a Business*. Reprinted with the permission of Simon & Schuster.
Copyright © 1987 by Paul Hawken.

Excerpts from Peter Binzen and Joseph Daughen, *The Wreck of the Penn Central.* Copyright © 1971
by Peter Binzen and Joseph Daughen. By permission of Little, Brown and Company.

Every reasonable effort has been made to trace owners of copyright materials in this book, but in
some instances this has proven impossible. The author and publisher will be glad to receive information leading to more complete acknowledgments in subsequent printings of the book and in the
meantime extend their apologies for any omissions.

To the women in my life—
Rosemary, Katherin, and Hannah

Contents

Introduction

About thirty years ago, American business schools commissioned a report by prominent academics regarding the status of business education in the United States. The report suggested that business was being taught too much as a trade—like plumbing, automotive mechanics, or tool and die making. Greater prestige and recognition would be accorded management education if it became more "professional," like medicine and law, and more "scientific," like physics or chemistry (see Gordon and Howell 1959; Pierson 1959).

The study hit home. Like most academics, American business educators did not want to be relegated to the status of mere "craftsmen" (people who produce unambiguous, practical products using skills acquired through long experience and the emulation of accomplished practitioners). The image of the "professional" (a person who produces ambiguous and sometimes esoteric products by attempting to apply scientific principles recorded in books) was much more appealing.

So the business schools professionalized, generating scientific principles and books in great profusion and relegating experience and emulation of practitioners to secondary concern. They were successful in these efforts, and the prestige of U.S. business schools became great indeed.

Meanwhile, the Japanese and Germans, without the benefit of a single business school rivaling the fame of a Harvard or even a Northwestern or Vanderbilt, are posed to take the place of the United States as the premier forces of Western capitalism. Perhaps not coincidentally, their success comes largely from the manufacture of unambiguous, practical products arising from a strong craft tradition buttressed by rigorous training in mathematics and basic science.

Of course, the blame for American industrial decline cannot be laid solely at the door of any one institution, much less the business schools, whose impact is probably far smaller than anyone would care to admit.

However, as a professor of management with a modicum of practical inclination, I am increasingly uncomfortable with a field that tends toward ever-greater theoretical sophistication, with diminishing concern for practice. The ideas of academics have had comparatively little impact on the practice of management, and much business school research actually trails after the lead of practicing managers. (See, for instance, Barley et al. 1988, a study of the evolution of academic research on corporate culture.) Thus, the major managerial fads (with their ubiquitous acronyms) such as Management by Objectives (MBO), Quality Control Circles (QC circles), Continuous Improvement, Total Quality Management (TQM), and Reengineering originate with practicing managers and are subsequently studied by academics without producing much that transcends the original formulations of practitioners.

The utility of much management research and theory is particularly limited in smaller organizations. Portfolio theory and much other strategic management thought is of little help to most single-product-line businesses. Similarly, most contemporary thinking about organizational structure and design grew out of research with large corporations. Even the techniques of less esoteric areas such as compensation, job analysis, and job design are of somewhat limited application in smaller organizations.

Their ivory-tower orientation notwithstanding, the business schools are populated by some very bright people, and they haven't been sitting on their hands. It takes a tremendous amount of sustained effort coupled with considerable intelligence and inventiveness to get tenure at a leading business school nowadays. Much of this work is of very limited practical applicability, but some of these efforts almost inadvertently have produced ideas and techniques with great practical potential. Unfortunately, these contributions have largely gone unappreciated and unused by practitioners because of academia's fixation on conceptual sophistication and unrealistic rigor coupled with neglect of practical considerations.

The purpose of this book is to adapt and present a number of ideas and techniques from the technical literature in a way that makes them useful to practicing businesspersons—particularly those of firms with less than three hundred employees. These represent the vast majority of organizations and those responsible for most economic growth in the United States.

Thus my major aim is to provide practicing managers and those who work with them access to useful tools that they would not otherwise possess. A secondary aim is to show academics how technical material can be adapted for practical use in the field. I hope also that some of the real-world experiences discussed herein will enhance theoretical discussion and debate.

Most of the material in this book is diagnostic in one way or another. Rarely will I tell you what to do in a given situation, but rather, how to find out what to do. I focus on diagnostics for three reasons. First, the technical literature produced by business schools is typically strongest in its diagnostic implications. Second, I believe that practicing managers, especially in smaller firms, are typically too heavy on action and light on diagnosis. Finally, I am skittish about proposing solutions, especially cookbook type solutions, because they so seldom work in one context in the same way they worked in another (Wheatly 1992). A good diagnostic process, on the other hand, usually suggests solutions that are molded to the peculiarities and specific needs of the organization diagnosed. These solutions may be superficially similar to those used by other organizations, but the process by which they are developed and implemented are unique and critical to their working in a specific organization (Schon 1983).

In choosing and presenting material I walk a fine line between simplifying to the point of doing violence to the original and retaining important concepts that are rather complex. When questions have arisen, I have opted for simplicity where possible, some complexity where necessary, and occasionally omission. My guide in these decisions has been the enhancement of craftsmanship. That is, if the idea or technique is practical, intuitive, helps me to understand my experience in the organization better, and seems to enhance my abilities with use, I have included it. If it is more complex than practical, if it is nonintuitive, and if it does not pay increasing dividends with repetition, I have not selected it for this volume.

Topics Covered

The above criteria plus the accidents of my own professional training and experience have resulted in the inclusion of the following topics in this book:

The GBAS Model of Organization

Academics are strongest in theory building. Entire journals are devoted to the development of theory, and some professors spend their entire work lives doing nothing but dreaming up theory. Managers care less for theory, not because theory is not useful, but because theorists do not tell them how it can be used. Theorists do not teach application because they themselves don't know how to apply theory. Nuclear fission and fusion would be impossible without Einstein's theory of relativity, but Einstein himself couldn't make an atomic bomb; it took a small army of scientists and engineers working together to figure that out. I have spent several years attempting to adapt organization theory for practical use, so my first contribution is to present a compact theory of organization and show my readers how it can be applied to concrete business situations. In my estimation, this is by far the most useful part of the book.

Organizational Dysfunctions

Informally, practicing managers know that bad things happen to organizations. Abundant folklore and colorful sayings about trying to drain the swamp when it is full of alligators attest to this. There is, however, little formal study of why things go wrong in organizations. It is as if we all whisper in the halls about problems and screwups, but few have the courage to discuss pathologies openly. Not unlike child abuse twenty years ago, everyone knows it exists but it is considered impolite to admit the fact in public.

I spend a chapter discussing the maladies that afflict organizations and giving them formal names. While this will not keep dysfunctions from happening, it at least provides some early warning and lets you know what you're up against. That is often half the battle.

Organizational Culture.   In a laudable study of *Fortune 500* companies that combines sound theory with a practical orientation, Kotter and Heskett (1992) found that corporations with healthy, adaptive cultures outperformed those with less appropriate values by hundreds of percent. Managers knew long before academics that organizations tend to have unique personalities or "cultures" of their own and that these cultures influence a host of things. However, this knowledge remained largely intuitive and anecdotal until consultants and academics began to exploit the commercial and scholarly value of the idea in the late 1970s. Most of this work has been done in large organizations with complex, many-faceted cultures that are normally very hard to change. This work has also catered to organizations with deep enough pockets to afford rather intensive, protracted studies.

Smaller organizations are less challenging culturally, both to diagnose and to change, but work on culture has not dealt with them specifically. There is a particular dearth of work proposing techniques for organizations with limited time and resources. In this book I offer three relatively simple techniques that enable those with limited time and money to analyze their cultures quickly and cheaply.

Social Networks.   Like culture, studies of organization structure have been fixated on bigness and complexity (see, for instance, the classical treatises of Blau and Scott 1962 and Hall 1991). Indeed, the major representations of organization structure, the organization chart, and the dimensions of horizontal and vertical differentiation, span of control, formalization, and so on, are of very limited value in smaller organizations. Instead of formal structures, smaller organizations use more fluid arrangements and depend more on the styles and contacts of individual leaders in getting things done. Traditional conceptualizations of structure are also increasingly obsolete in today's volatile business environment.

For years, sociologists have used a technique called sociometry to study how informal social structures work. It is a Godsend for anyone wanting to know how organizations really work.

Sociometry, or social network analysis, has been used more frequently in analyzing relations between large organizations, but it can and has been used inside organizations. It is particularly well suited for figuring out what is going on socially in organizations that do not rely heavily on traditional formal managerial techniques. I have spent a large part of my career adapting this technique for practical use in organizations and will pay particular attention to its application in small organizations in this book.

Cause Maps.   A large part of everyday decisionmaking, for managers and nonmanagers alike, involves thinking about what causes what. Cognitive mapping or cause mapping is a relatively simple technique for graphically portraying and thinking about cause and effect. In a smaller organization, a good cause map can often capture the essence of the enterprise and what makes it tick. When the major players of a small firm provide input, a detailed record of the strategic thinking of the entire firm results. I dedicate a short chapter at the end of the book to explaining cause maps and showing how they can shed light on the dilemmas of small organizations.

There is an unmistakable propensity toward hyperbole and panaceas in papular management books. The words "revolutionary," "radical," "total," "fundamental," "comprehensive," "far reaching," and the like, are used, I think, far too often. Perhaps such superlatives are necessary to pry harried managers away from their immediate problems long enough to read and reflect. But I think that ultimately building and managing organizations is a slow, incremental, painstaking process. Hence, I have no big, messianic answers to managers' problems. I do offer some important tools for figuring out problems. Moreover, while I take pains to present things simply, you will have to read rather carefully and think about what you read to derive maximum benefit from this book. My choice of a title reflects the view that a good mechanic and a competent manager have a lot in common. Both need a basic understanding of what makes the thing work. Both need to be able to observe carefully and think rigorously about their observations. Both need to know what tends to go wrong in a given situation. Both need good tools. In sum, both need to be craftspeople. If you also see management as a craft to be perfected, you will find this book useful.

1

How Organizations Work
and How You Can Make
Your Organization Work Better

One of the joys of working with small organizations is rapid feedback. When I'm involved in reorganizing or trying to change a big company, it is seldom clear initially what was a good idea and what wasn't. Sometimes I never find out—the wheels turn too slowly, and causes and effects are filtered through too many different systems to really know. In small companies however, things are so interdependent—tightly coupled, as academics like to say (see Weick 1979)—that both mistakes and good moves show up rather quickly.

What is not always apparent is why mistakes are mistakes. We may see that the change in business hours was a flop, but it may be hard to tell why the early shoppers didn't materialize or the all-night-bar patrons chose to drink elsewhere. As managers try different approaches to their challenges and opportunities, they develop a memory of what specific things have worked or have flopped, and they develop intuitions about why. But these intuitions are rarely systematic, nor are they easily explained to others. As a result, practicing managers have difficulty transmitting their knowledge to others in the organization and may not be able to pinpoint and remedy deficiencies in their thinking, particularly when conditions change. (This is one reason why most organizations die with their founders: they are unable, unwilling, or too busy to pass on their intuition to successors; see Hodgetts 1988.)

Academics, on the other hand are trained to develop systematic, explicit models of how things work and to explain them to others. Unfortunately, they are usually more interested in debating the comparative virtues of these models and developing esoteric tests to confirm their truth than in applying them to real-life situations. They also have an irritating tendency to develop models that are more complex than the phenomena being studied. In this chapter, I will present a relatively simple model of organizations that I have found useful in understanding how institutions of all sizes work. It is particularly applicable to small organizations and very useful for tracking down causes when things don't work. I believe a formal model such as this, when coupled with the experience of the practicing manager, can be much more powerful and practical than either academic theory or business experience alone.

The components of the model are not original, but my particular combination and usage of these elements is my own. I apologize in advance to those luminaries whose work I may have misconstrued.

The GBAS Model of Organization

One of the most common definitions of organizations is a "group of people united by a common objective" (Hall 1976). While all organizations have objectives, it takes more than a common objective to make an organization. A mob of people looting a supermarket can be said to have a common objective, but they do not constitute an organization. (The cynic in me would have to say that I have seen organizations that seemed somewhat less organized than your average mob.) According to the model to be presented here, our looters need boundaries and an activity system before they can be called an organization, hence the acronym GBAS—Goal, Boundary, Activity System. (See Aldrich 1978 for more detail.)

The rioters do not have a systematic way of pursuing their objective; each person goes about the task at hand with no coordination, explicit methods, or regularity to guide their efforts. There are also no boundaries separating the rioters from their environment. It is hard to tell who is "in" or "out" of the mob. Anyone who happens along may join in with nothing except the common activity to distinguish the newcomer from other persons in the vicinity. Similarly, there is no definition of what objects, ideas, or other resources are "in" or "out" of the mob. It has no property, no ideology, and no way to tell where it ends and the rest of the world begins. Membership is fleeting and uncertain.

Goals

In contrast, organizations have all three components. All organizations have goals, even if ill-defined and unattained. Better organizations have a fairly sharp sense of where they are headed. The traditional definition of a goal as a "desired end state" is acceptable here, but for studying organizations I prefer a broader definition: A goal is that portion of the environment that the organization selects as its domain or turf. A simpler way of stating might be, "An organization's goal or domain is WHO it wants to serve." This broader definition lets me make use of some of the insights of those who study managerial strategy. (See Miles and Snow 1978, for instance.)

Although organizational domains can vary in a number of ways, two properties are particularly important: breadth and stability. Domain breadth refers to the number of different kinds of customers an organization seeks to serve. Hence, a hospital that treats both psychiatric and cancer patients has a broader domain than one which treats one or the other. Stability refers to how often the organization's environment changes. A cement factory with constant demand has a more stable domain than a computer manufacturer. A music company that publishes classics has a more stable domain than one that publishes popular music: and one that publishes both genres has a broader domain than a company that offers only one.

Boundaries

All organizations must maintain boundaries if they are to avoid dissolving into the environment. A boundary is anything that regulates the flow of ideas, people, matter, or energy into or out of the organization. Another way of defining boundaries is "What organizations use to attract or exclude things coming in and to limit or encourage things going out of the firm." Organizations maintain a bewildering array of boundaries. Hiring standards and guidelines regulate the conditions under which people in the environment become part of or depart from the organization. Prices regulate the conditions under which products leave the organization.

For anyone who has ever gone to college, boundaries are so extensive that the concept should be easy to grasp. For instance, entrance requirements determine under what conditions students can enter. Graduation requirements and tuition determine under what conditions students may honorably leave (smart and poor). Tuition, fees, and fines determine how much money must come in if the student is to graduate or maintain good standing, and so on.

In manufacturing organizations, finished product inspections regulate the exit of outputs from organizations generally. Raw material inspection regulates the flow of matter into the organizations, debt policies regulate capital inflows, and so on. The values an organization accepts are a very important boundary called culture, for which I have reserved an entire chapter.

Permeability is one of the more important ways that boundaries can vary. As the name suggests, permeability refers to how hard it is to get into and out of the organization. Harvard has quite impermeable boundaries, community colleges do not. Sometimes one organizational boundary will be permeable, but another will not. For instance, it is easy to get into prison but hard to get out. (However, I will argue later that uneven permeability is fairly unusual and often dangerous.)

Activity Systems

All organizations maintain activity systems. That is to say, all organizations have systematic, predictable ways of doing work. Thus we can think of the goal as "Who is served," boundaries as "What attracts, repels, admits, or retains them," and activity systems as "How the work gets done." Alternatively, the activity system can be defined as "How they are served." There is a bewildering variety of activity systems, but all organizations must somehow systematize their internal activities if they are to generate output. The activity system includes all mechanisms regulating and directing the internal affairs of the organization. Organization structure, internal boundaries, physical layout, and production methods are all components of the activity system.

Two important ways that activity systems can vary are their complexity and flexibility. Simple activity systems have few components which are not very different from one another. Complex activity systems have many diverse components. Flexible activity systems adapt to changes and nonstandard requests quickly and gracefully, while inflexible activity systems have difficulty dealing with change and variation. All other things being equal, simpler activity systems are more flexible than complex ones. On the other hand, complex activity systems are usually more efficient than simple ones.

Information, people, matter, and energy are constantly passing through the boundaries of the organization, where they are processed by the activity system and sent back through the boundaries into the environment. Incoming things are usually called inputs, outgoing things are called outputs (Katz and Kahn 1978), and movement of inputs or outputs through the organization are called flows. Figure 1.1 contains a summary of the GBAS model of organization.

A Backyard Organization

I believe the above definition succinctly captures much of what must happen in any organization if it is to survive. I have found it very useful in understanding how organizations compete and in identifying some of the things that go wrong in organizations. To show how the model works in practice, see Figure 1.1.

When I lived in Brazil, I had an acquaintance who operated a small factory in his back yard. (This is not uncommon in Brazil; it cuts down on commuting and rent.) Refer to Figure 1.2 for a diagram of his production facilities. The factory had three employees. One worker (Number 1 in the figure) spent his time with a rubber mallet and machete, cutting discarded off-road tires into small squares of uniform thickness. A second worker placed these squares on a lathe and transformed them into circles. The third

Figure 1.1   Summary of GBAS Model

Goal/Domain:	Who we serve		
	Attribute:	Breadth:	Range of different customers
	Options:	Broad–narrow	
		Stability:	Rate of change in customer needs and products that fulfill those needs
	Options:	Stable–unstable	
Boundaries:	What attracts/repels		
	Attribute:	Permeability:	Ease of entry or exit of ideas, people, energy, material, etc.
	Options:	Permeable–impermeable	
Activity System:	How work is done (how inputs get to be outputs)		
	Attributes:	Complexity:	The number of different elements
	Options:	Simple–complex	
		Flexibility:	Ease of change
	Options:	Inflexible–flexible	

worker made several holes in the circle, using a round metal guide or jig indicating where he should drill. He then used a grinder to remove any irregularities and smooth the piece, which he deposited in a cardboard box.

Every two weeks or so, the owner would appear to count and inspect the finished product. If he considered the workers' production sufficient in number and quality, he would multiply the number of pieces by three different values and pay each worker. If production was substandard, he would discharge the presumed offender, contract another, and depart as suddenly as he came.

Even in this rudimentary description of this rudimentary organization, we can identify boundaries and elements of an activity system. Recall that boundaries regulate the entrance and exit of people, matter, energy, or ideas. We note that although my friend did not appear overly discriminating as to the quality of his raw material (discarded tires were acceptable), he evidently stipulated that one general type of tire (the off-road type used in strip mining and road building) be used. The requirement that only off-road tires be used as raw material is therefore an input boundary. We note also that only people who attained the stipulated levels of production and quality were retained in the organization. Hence, his production standards constitute a boundary because they regulate the entrance of people into the organization (or at least their permanence).

Figure 1.2   Backyard Enterprises

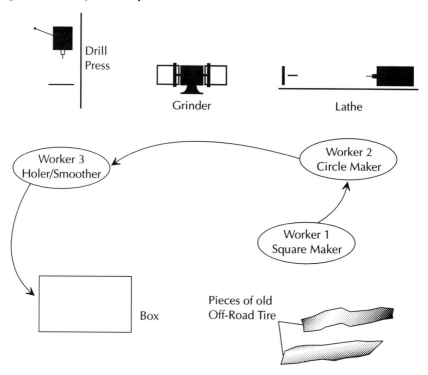

Most of the identifiable boundaries could be construed as lax or permeable. Entrance boundaries for raw material and labor were relatively undiscriminating. I am aware of no thorough inspection of the discarded tires or detailed testing of job applicants. There are other indications of permeability. The lathe and other equipment were bought used, and the firm was heavily in debt. The owner used income from the firm for personal purposes and financed operations out of bank loans. Here we see minimal discrimination regarding what kind of equipment and what kind of money entered the organization.

The activity system is easier to identify, perhaps because the flow of raw material through the system is easy to trace. Indeed, tracing the flow of inputs through the organization is a good way to identify and analyze an activity system. Raw material goes through four fixed production steps (squaring, circling, holing, and smoothing) that never vary. These steps are divided between three people who never change tasks. A metal pattern is used to control the drilling process. The physical position of the tools is fixed, as is the sequence of production steps. Of the many, perhaps less efficient, ways the disks could have been made, this organization has one system with five steps that never change.

Examining this activity system, the words "simple" and "rigid" probably come to mind. Our first impressions are right on the second count but wrong on the first. The activity system is indeed rigid inasmuch as tasks and production steps remain the same and changing any of them would prove disruptive. However, if we define complexity as the number of different elements in a system, we would have to conclude that for the product it makes, this activity system is rather complex. Remember that separate, distinct jobs exist for making squares and circles, and another job exists for making holes and smoothing. The simplest activity system would be to have one person carrying out all the operations. This would of course require one person to have a command of all production steps. The most complex system possible would involve splitting person 3's job into two separate holing and smoothing jobs. Note that, all other things being equal, the more complex the activity system, the less complex the individual job, and vice versa.

There is nothing in the above description that impresses us regarding the quality of this organization's management. On the contrary, one gets the image of a rather laid back, fly-by-night operation. If it were a service station, we would expect the rest rooms to be dirty. It may come as a surprise, therefore, that this company was competing head to head with multinationals and beating them handily in efficiency, price, and profit margins.

The reason for this success is the perfect fit this organization had forged between environment, goals, boundaries, and activity system. Of course, you cannot know this because we have not yet discussed the firm's goals. Indeed, until you know an organization's goals, you cannot accurately diagnose boundaries or activity systems, because the optimal form these should take is dictated by who the organization is trying to serve or, as I would say, by the organization's domain.

The Domain of Backyard Enterprises

In the rugged hills of central Brazil, the twisted roads are often riddled with potholes caused by tropical rains and heavy traffic. This means that vehicles, especially heavily laden trucks, frequently damage their leaf springs. Frequent tire and undercarriage damage has stimulated the proliferation of small repair shops on particularly bad stretches of highway. When leaf springs are broken, the bushing that goes between the spring and mounting pin must also be replaced, and replacement bushings from the original manufacturer are quite expensive.

By manufacturing bushings in his own backyard using scrap rubber and unskilled labor, our friend fills the needs of a small market very efficiently.

No one sees the bushings after they are installed, so aesthetics are not important, and a stranded truck driver is in little position to insist on original parts, even if he is convinced that they are better than the backyard variety. The original manufacturer must maintain an inventory of all of a truck's parts, and this generates enormous overhead and inventory costs.

Because of their size and visibility, the original equipment manufacturers are scrupulously audited by the Brazilian IRS. All original manufacturer's sales, therefore, are duly recorded using standard bookkeeping practices. Moreover, even if scrapped off-road tires were adequate raw material, their use would not likely enhance the reputation of the manufacturer.

Our backyard friend, on the other hand, has almost no overhead, little inventory, and virtually no packaging costs. He need not second guess the aftermarket for his product. He simply takes orders every few weeks when he makes deliveries. And of course his prices are lower.

Although we have no formal goal statement for this firm, we may infer from the facts described what the goal of the organization is. Indeed, this process usually renders a more accurate description of the "real" goals than any written statement: and in and of itself it is a useful diagnostic exercise. Ask yourself, "If we had to rely on acts rather than words to identify our goals, what would they be?" From the facts here we infer that our friend's goal is to provide isolated repair shops with a very limited variety of bushings that will fit on certain trucks that break their springs out in the country. The parts must be cheaper than the original manufacturer's parts and must be invisible to tax inspectors.

Organizational boundaries and activity system match this narrow and stable domain perfectly. The goal requires only minimal quality and product variety, and the organizational boundaries supply raw materials and labor inputs in a way that provides no more nor less than is absolutely necessary. The activity system is set up in such a manner that unskilled labor produces acceptable results with minimal capital and almost no supervision. Thus this firm has successfully dodged the two perennial dysfunctions in management—the tendency to carry out unnecessary activity and the inability to differentiate between necessary and unnecessary activities.

So What?: Applying the Model

You are now in possession of a rudimentary theory of organizations and its application to one real-life setting. This is a step on our journey, but only a step. At this point you may have some inkling of how this model of organizations may prove useful, but it is probably not much more than a glimmer. I could now discuss further theoretical aspects or practical applications of the model, but that would be premature. Ultimately, the model's utility will become largely self-evident, but only after you become fully conversant with it. The reason for this is that the utility of any tool and how to use it—be it a set of chopsticks or a mass spectrometer—is never clear when you first put your hands on it. Because you are not yet on intimate terms with the model in a real-life context, illustrations of its practical application would be difficult to grasp and quickly forgotten.

Therefore, my task now is to make you so comfortable with this model that you will have difficulty *not* seeing organizations as agglomerations of goals, boundaries, and activity systems. The normal way of doing this is through exercises applying the tool to a given medium. Having read a score or more of books containing ingenious, illuminating exercises and never having completed a single one, I know better. Instead, I will walk you through an exercise that someone else has already completed, knowing that the impulse to look at your neighbor's paper is forever strong, even for those who left school decades ago. Once the exercise is completed, it will be easier to extend the model and explore its practical implications. The exercise involves several steps:

A GBAS Exercise

1. Choose two competing or at least two comparable organizations (McDonald's and Burger King are used here).
2. Make a list of at least fifty tangible, observable, or independently verifiable differences that distinguish them from each other.
3. Classify the differences as belonging to the organizations' boundaries or activity systems. Leave the domain or goals for later.
4. Classify the two organizations' boundaries (permeability) and activity system (complexity and flexibility). Defend your statements with facts from your list.
5. Try to infer the goals from the boundaries. Classify the domains as broader versus narrower, and more versus less stable.

This exercise, if done correctly, will result in three or four pages of text, but it is not difficult writing. First comes the list of differences:

McDonald's	Burger King
Burgers fried	Burgers flame broiled
No onion rings	Onion rings
Has one line for each cash register	Has only one line for whole restaurant
Serves sundaes	No sundaes
Greater total number of menu items	Fewer menu items
Frequent Saturday morning TV ads	Fewer Saturday ads
Ronald McDonald and friends	Had an effete king monarch, now retired

McDonald's	Burger King
Uses warming rack to store unsold product	No warming rack apparent
Makes burgers before orders are made	Tends to wait for order and then assemble sandwich
Faster service for standard orders	Slow service for most orders
Slower service for special orders	Faster service for special orders
Many booths	Few booths
More suburban locations	More central locations
Bigger bathrooms	More one-holers
More play facilities	Fewer play facilities
Two drive-through windows	One drive-through window
Larger parking lots	Fewer parking spaces
More doors	Fewer doors
Several registers	One or two registers
Server gets drinks	Customer gets own drink
Average meal somewhat cheaper	Average meal more expensive
Wait for your meal	Will bring you your order
Burgers fried in lots	Burgers fried on conveyer
No ceiling fans	Ceiling fans
Brighter colors	Subdued colors
Emphasize package meals	Less emphasis on package meals
Caters birthday parties	Doesn't cater parties
Same person takes money, fills order	Different people take money, fill order
Different people fry burgers, prepare buns, and wrap product	Same person assembles and packages burger
Serves pizza	No pizza
Serves fajitas	No fajitas
Standardized greeting	No standard greeting
Serves ice cream cones	No ice cream cones
Happy meals a major product	Kids' meals a recent addition
Cooking and assembly not visible	Cooking visible
Breakfast buffet	No breakfast buffet

Classification.   Having completed the list (step one), step two is to classify observations as to boundary or activity system. Although it is ultimately a judgment call which is which, considerable confusion can be avoided by asking "Does this item deal principally with how work is executed or with how inputs are attracted and outputs are regulated?" The fact that McDonald's offers both pizza and hamburgers obviously will make numerous demands on the activity system. Just knowing that pizza is sold does not tell us how the pizza-making work is done. It does, however, suggest that people wanting both pizza and hamburgers, or not yet know-ing which they want, will be more attracted to McDonald's than to Burger King. Hence, we classify pizza offering as a boundary feature. Moreover, it is a boundary feature that creates more permeability for McDonald's than for Burger King.

The fact that you get your own drink at Burger King is a harder call. It means that BK employees don't have to serve drinks, making the activity system slightly less complex—it contains one fewer task. On the other hand, it also means that refills are free, so that once you have paid for your cup, there is no further regulation of soda leaving the company. This clearly makes for a more permeable exit boundary in that regard. Therefore, the "get your own drink" fact qualifies as both, although the best way to han-dle such a fact is to split it into two facts:

1. The customer pays a flat fee for all the soda he can drink—a (perme-able) boundary.
2. The customer fetches his own drink—a (simplifying) aspect of the ac-tivity system.

Once determinations are made as to which facts describe boundaries and which describe the activity system, it is best to physically rearrange the lists so that boundaries and activity systems from the two competitors can be re-viewed as units. (In the interest of space I have not done this third step here.) Alternatively, you can mark boundary items with B's and activity-sys-tem items with A's.

Step Four.   If steps two and three have been done well, step four, where goals and boundaries are typified, should be easy and illuminating. In the case at hand it is quite obvious that McDonald's has much more permeable boundaries and a much more complex activity system than Burger King. On the boundary side, McDonald's is easier to get into and out of by virtue of its location, parking facilities, number of doors, speed of service, number of registers, lower prices, and even its larger restrooms. It is easier to fre-quent McDonald's in groups with mixed tastes and demographics because of its more diverse menu offerings, play facilities, and catering.

Burger King is harder to get to, harder to park at, takes longer to be served, costs more, and so on, making its boundaries generally higher (i.e., less perme-able). The activity systems of the two organizations are not quite as obvious as the boundaries, mostly because much of the activity system is proprietary and out of view of the casual observer. Even so, it is quite clear that the activity system at McDonald's is more complex (i.e., it has more diverse components) than Burger King's. McDonald's has at least four more distinct job functions than Burger King when one considers frying, prepping, packaging, and getting drinks. And this does not even consider catering parties and preparing other menu items, like pizza, that Burger King does not offer.

Note again that the more complex activity system at McDonald's does not mean that individual jobs are more complex. On the contrary, if other things like the variety of menu items are held constant, more complex activity systems result in simpler jobs. At Burger King you must know how to prep and wrap all the different sandwiches, and you must keep track of who wants onions but no mayonnaise and vice versa. At McDonald's, you just fry, or you just prep, or you just wrap standard products.

Of course, having a simpler activity system with more complex jobs makes it possible to be more flexible; it is much easier to keep track of who doesn't want mayonnaise if you don't have to keep track of who doesn't want anchovies on their pizza, too. Hence, McDonald's has a complex, inflexible activity system that produces a wide variety of standardized items, while Burger King has a simple, flexible activity system that produces a smaller variety of customized (or at least customizable) items. Despite the many similarities between McDonald's and Burger King, a more fundamental difference in boundaries and activity systems between two competitors in the same industry would be hard to imagine.

Step Five.   Step five of the exercise requires that we infer the two firms' domains from their boundaries. Again, this is straightforward if our observations have been numerous and objective. All we need ask is "Who would be attracted by the boundaries observed thus far?" In the McDonald's case, hints are legion. Ronald McDonald, playland, happy meals, Saturday morning TV ads, and catered birthday parties all should attract children, which by default will bring their parents.

More subtle are boundaries that appeal more directly to parents. Parents can herd children into a booth and keep them there by stationing an adult on either end. Waiting for food with children is exquisite torture, so speedy service is of the essence. Children take forever to make up their minds, and a standardized happy meal shortens the agony. (Moreover, the plastic toy can be held hostage against food eaten, and the puzzles on the box occupy childrens' attention.) By the same token, harried parents don't want to think about menu selections while their children squirm and fight, so the emphasis on "value meal" packages where the only choices are between Coke and Sprite is again useful. Children constantly need to eliminate or be cleaned (often in close succession), so restrooms are critical. Price is important because there are always at least two diners, and usually more, involved when a child is present.

Not for the Faint Hearted: Children at Burger King.   Who will be attracted by Burger King's boundaries is a little harder to divine. The chain makes sporadic overtures to children, but any parent who has taken children to Burger King knows that several boundaries are not highly compatible. Upon entering, the child immediately mistakes the entry maze for a balance beam or parallel bars, much to the chagrin of the parent and the alarm of the manager—not to mention the shins and calves of other customers. After agonizing over what to order and asking repeatedly when the food will be ready, the children discover the joys of the soda fountain, where Coke can be mixed with Sprite and orange drink.

Once the child's cup runneth over, the magical rumbling of the ice machine is detected and copious quantities of ice splash into the already full cup, sending carbonated fructose into the hair and clothing of the child and nearby patrons. The family is then seated at adjacent individual tables with those swinging chairs that were designed for the removal of small fingers. I could go on, but the point has been made.

If parents wanting a fast, predictable variety of standardized food and easy management of their progeny are not BK's domain, what is? Again, we ask "Who would be attracted by Burger King's particular boundaries?" That is, who would be attracted by a burger prepared to order, costing a little bit more, taking a little more time, without the options of pizza, fajitas, soup, or sundaes? Who doesn't need large restrooms, suburban or interstate locations, large booths, or playgrounds, but would like unlimited refills and wouldn't mind having their burgers brought to them?

The Burger King Client. With some imagination, we can develop a profile of the likely patron. As predicted above, this person is less likely to be eating with a small child or children. He has a little more money and time to spend on a meal and has rather definite, even esoteric, tastes. He knows what he wants before coming to the establishment and will seek out an establishment specializing in pizza or fish or hamburgers in order to satisfy these tastes, rather than choosing an all-purpose outlet that will please a party uncritical about specific dishes but divided on what to eat. At eating time he is more likely to be downtown than in the suburbs, or has the leisure and inclination to drive to a slightly less accessible location.

We are, of course, speaking of the childless adult or postpubescent teenager. Alternately, we may be speaking of the adult with children who is eating out for lunch or who has absconded from the domestic unit to eat lunch in relative peace. This is the kind of person who still may indulge in the myth that you can "have it your way." (People with children know that you not only can't have it your way, you're lucky to get it at all.)

The fact that the same patrons may occasionally belong to two organizational domains should not be a cause of consternation; this is a common fact of capitalist life. I occasionally drive my '78 Chevy to a fancy restaurant, and occasionally a Jaguar turns up at a McDonald's parking lot. But, it is important for organizations to choose and signal their domain clearly.

Finally, to finish our exercise, we identify the nature of the two competitors' domains. Several things identify McDonald's domain as broader than Burger King's. The fact that it seeks both children and their parents adds breadth, as does the variety of menu items. Clearly, the more generic nature of McDonald's targets a broader cross section of the population at more disparate occasions in life. These occasions may range from picking up dinner on the way home, to a birthday party with the kids, to turning off the interstate for morning caffeine and a newspaper. Moreover, as is almost unavoidable for organizations with broad domains, McDonald's domain is less stable. Witness the frequent new-product introductions and constant experimentation that characterize the chain.

Burger King, on the other hand, is content either to wait for individual adults to decide that it is hamburger day or to remind them with coupons in the newspaper (the one place children never look).

What We Have Learned from the Exercise

Hopefully, the dry bones of our model are now slowly starting to get up and walk around (Biblical illiterates, check Ezekiel for an explanation of the "dry bones" metaphor). A number of important attributes of organizations should be occurring to you now, thanks to the GBAS model. You may even be able to see some ways this model can be used to explain or improve an organization that is dear to you. To consolidate your insights, let's look at some interesting regularities from our McDonald's/Burger King adventure, as summarized à la GBAS.

	McDonald's	*Burger King*
Goal/Domain		
Breadth	Broad	Narrow
Stability	Unstable	Stable
Boundaries		
Permeability	Permeable	Impermeable
Activity system		
Complexity	Complex	Simple
Flexibility	Inflexible	Flexible

If you look very long and very hard at the chart above you will begin to see that, deconstructionsts and thrivers on chaos notwithstanding, there is some order in the organizational universe. Specifically, four facts of organizational life become apparent:

1. There is fit.
2. Things come in packages.
3. There are opposites.
4. There are trade-offs.

There Is Fit.   In our example of the backyard factory, we noted with admiration the tight fit between the elements of my friend's organization and the environment within which he operated. Again, here, we find extraordinary fit between the elements of each organization. The complex, subdivided activity system at McDonald's permits a variety of standard menu items to be prepared quickly and cheaply, which perfectly fits the wants of the harried parents and impatient children whom the chain has chosen as its domain.

Burger King's simpler, less diverse activity system permits a small number of fresh, customized menu items to be prepared somewhat more leisurely, and at somewhat greater expense. This in turn fits the needs of the somewhat less harried, more munificent adults that are BK's target market.

Fit is an indispensable fact of life. Imagine the pandemonium that would ensue under the golden arches if, some lunch time, the manager decided to make everything to order. And imagine the wrath of the postpubescent individualist who some dark day dismounts from his Harley at Burger King only to be told that he must eat his Whopper with pickles or not at all.

Things Come in Packages.   It is noteworthy how almost all of the boundaries of McDonald's are more permeable than its competitor, and vice versa. It has more doors, more drive-in windows, lower prices, more convenient locations, faster service, more menu items, and so on. All of these elements make it easy to get in and out of the organization. This consistency between boundary mechanisms (and components of the activity system, for that matter) is an important indicator of good management, just like fit between the elements of the organization.

Considerable inefficiencies can occur if an element doesn't fit into its package. Think of a McDonald's with only two cash registers, or think of a Wal-Mart downtown with no parking. Or think of a fancy restaurant with ketchup in little packages instead of bottles. It just does not work.

Occasionally an organization can profit by having some boundaries permeable while others are impermeable, but it is a dangerous practice that can confuse customers and it should only be undertaken cautiously as part of a well-planned strategy.

There Are Opposites.   Note how the strength of one competitor—say, Burger King's freshness and customization—are the weakness of the other—witness McDonald's standardization and sometimes cold burgers. Indeed, as we go down the GBAS list of organizational components, we find that Burger King is a mirror image of McDonald's. This is probably not accidental. Fairly few organizations compete head to head and live to tell about it. This does not mean they do not have comparable models and serve comparable markets: firms in the same industry must all look to the same finite population of customers in choosing a domain. But surviving firms typically compete by capitalizing on areas where their main competitor is weak.

In the case of Burger King there was probably very little choice as to the domain it should choose. Because McDonald's was the first truly mammoth burger franchise, it was able to carve out a huge domain by catering to families on the basis of price, speed, convenient location, and standardization. As a later entrant to the market, Burger King did not have the real estate holdings, the massive economies of scale in purchasing and procurement, and years of finetuning their activity system and boundaries to make an efficiently produced standard product that would appeal to the largest cross section of the population possible.

Instead it had to find a segment of the population for which McDonald's strengths are weaknesses. In retrospect, at least, it would seem obvious that offering a nonstandard (i.e., customized) product to a nonfamily population would be the only real option. Once this decision is made, everything else falls into place. And the places that everything falls into are the exact opposite of the dominant competitor—singles not families, customization not standardization, higher quality not lower price, fresher not faster, specialty menu rather than a catchall menu, and so on.

Such opposites are found in most competitive situations. Henry Ford revolutionized the industry by introducing a cheap standardized car. William Durrant of General Motors competed with Ford by producing a "car for every purse and purpose"—in other words by offering more varied models at higher prices. Federal Express moves smaller packages very quickly; UPS moves larger packages less quickly. The Soviet armed forces relied on enormous weapons and great numbers of personnel; the U.S. armed forces have stressed flexibility, training, and technological innovation instead of size and numbers. Wal-Mart has stressed low prices and name brands; Kmart traditionally has stressed amenities and house brands.

There Are Trade-Offs.   For all except the most utopian, there should be little doubt by now that you can't be a McDonald's and a Burger King at the same time. Like life in general, business is full of trade-offs; and the manager who pretends they don't exist does so at her peril. A number of trade-offs are illustrated in our exercise. These, as well as several others, will surface again and again in this book. To reiterate a few: speed versus customization, quality versus price, flexibility versus efficiency, permeability versus simplicity.

Applying the Theory: How to Use the GBAS Model to Avoid Being Fried (or Flame Broiled) by Your Competition

I believe that a deep understanding of these four facts of organizational life will make you a wise manager. For some reason, though, managers never come to me asking to be made wise. Instead they come to me for "practical solutions," "bottom line impact," "hands on advice," "step by step instructions," and "things I can do right away." (This is unfortunate, for if they were to come seeking wisdom once or twice, they wouldn't have to come back constantly for solutions.)

But I suppose it is unrealistic to expect managers to spend their time pondering the cosmos when the proverbial swamp is full of alligators. Therefore I now offer a few "step by step instructions for generating practical, hands-on solutions that you can implement today to impact your bottom line," using the GBAS model. Basically, the steps outlined below adapt the exercise you read above to diagnosing your own competitive fitness and that of your major competitor. (You can use it to analyze more than one competitor if you wish.) It uses the "things come in packages" principle to estimate likely characteristics of your competition that you otherwise would not know. It also applies the "there must be fit" and "there are opposites" principles to suggest how you can best position yourself vis-à-vis your competition and what specific things in your organization need to be changed. If you will go through the steps below religiously once, or preferably twice, a year, you should be able to out-manage if not out-perform most competitors.

Step 1: Determine Your Domain.

This step is similar to Peter Drucker's shopworn but excellent question "What business are we in?" Ask yourself "Who are we trying to serve?" or "What is our turf?" Be specific. And don't go to your files for a profile of your typical customer. Some domain statements might be:

- Our title company primarily wants to serve brokers who close commercial real estate transactions in the Portland metropolitan area, and secondarily residential transactions above $100,000.
- Our club wants to serve people who prefer to dance to a variety of country music in a nonalcoholic environment.

- Our practice wants to primarily serve professional Jewish couples and their children who have psychological challenges that don't require institutionalization.

Step 1: This step should be done by the CEO of the organization. Subsequent steps should be done by someone else.

Step 2: Make a list of at least fifty factual differences between you and your most important competitor, just as was done for the McDonald's/Burger King exercise.

This time, however, add to your list at least fifteen things you know about yourself that you don't know about your closest competitor.

Step 3: Classify the differences as belonging to the organizations' boundaries or activity systems. Leave blanks for information not known about your competitor.

Step 4: Classify the two organizations' boundaries (permeability) and activity system (complexity and flexibility). Defend your statements with facts from your list.

Step 5: Try to infer the goals from the boundaries (independent of step one carried out by the CEO). Classify the domains as broader versus narrower, more versus less stable.

Step 6: Try to guess the fifteen unknown attributes of you competitor identified in step one.

This step is possible because of the third fact of life of organizations listed above: Things come in packages. Once you have some idea of the activity system, boundaries, and domain of an organization, your understanding of the relationship between elements and your knowledge that elements tend to fit into related packages will make it possible to formulate accurate guesses about unknown aspects of that organization.

For instance, we know that the McDonald's activity system is more complex and rigid than Burger King's, but we know nothing about either firm's human resource boundaries. We do know, however, that McDonald's boundaries are generally more permeable. The facts we know lead us to speculate that Burger King might have less permeable human resource boundaries—slightly higher pay, more careful selection, more hours per employee, and somewhat lower turnover.

Step 7: Ask embarrassing questions.

The following worksheet can be your guide.

Question 1. How closely are the CEO's description of the domain and the inferences about your domain derived from the study of boundaries and activity systems?

Very Close   1   2   3   4   5   Very Distant

Considerable distance between the official domain and the inferred domain indicates that something does not fit. To remedy this, review each component of the activity system and ask how it does or does not fit the domain. For instance, if a restaurant includes personnel from neighboring offices in its domain, it may need to adjust its serving time to the typical lunch hour or offer lunch delivery to make its boundaries more permeable. If a gun shop wants to attract first-time buyers, it may want to offer introductory shooting classes.

Question 2. How close are the domains of our organization and its leading competitor?

Very Close   1   2   3   4   5   Very Distant

If the two domains are very close, and your market is not growing rapidly, you face the possibility of ruinous head-to-head competition. In this case, you need to realistically assess your strengths and weaknesses and decide either to differentiate your approach or consider buying, selling, or driving your competitor out of business. The more likely course would be to broaden or narrow the domain to be strong where your competitor is weak. For instance, if your competitor is the low-cost producer of row houses, maybe you should increase your customizing capability. If the bar down the street attracts traditional wealth, maybe you can attract new wealth. (Alternatively, if the bar down the street attracts traditional poverty, perhaps you can attract new poverty.)

If the two domains are very distant, it is probably worthwhile to become a little more aggressive. So if your chief competitor has been installing a lot of air conditioners in new housing and you have been working only with existing units, it may be time to make some overtures to major builders in your area. Or if your competitor seems to be delivering a lot of pizzas to the university dorms and your delivery orders come mostly from single-family dwellings, it may be worth the investment to put some coupons in the student newspaper around finals time.

Question 3: Who has the tightest fit between goals, boundaries, and activity system?

You   1   2   3   4   5   Your Competitor

To answer this question, take each element in your boundary and ask whether it fits the activity system. Then take each element in your boundary and ask if it fits the domain. Although most of the fit with goals comes through the boundaries, try also to assess the fit directly between domain and elements in the activity system. Now repeat the process for your competitor.

A number of subtle disjunctures may appear, all of which reduce your effectiveness. For example, a blue-collar restaurant may find its acceptance of credit cards does little to attract customers from its domain. Conversely, an auto repair shop near an interstate may be losing business because it doesn't take American Express; at the same time, it is getting business it doesn't want because of too-liberal credit terms to poor locals.

If analysis of your major competitor suggests very loose fit, and your firm is tightly managed, a vigorous incursion into the competitor's domain is much more likely to be successful than if both companies are about the same. If your competitor features a better fit, then you'd better differentiate your domain from hers a little more and work on tightening your ship.

Step 8: Write down all of the possible changes and adjustments suggested by step seven.

Make sure they are all stated in terms that are sufficiently precise for you to know when they have been accomplished. For example: "Phase out credit for customers making less that $900 a month," or "Secure a toll-free number to make customer inquiries easier." Decide which of these things can be done within the next six months and assign specific individuals responsibility for doing them.

Step 9: Repeat the study (the second time goes much faster) in six months and check up on the measures that were supposed to be taken.

2

Dysfunctions: Awful Things That Happen to Organizations

In the first chapter we discussed how organizations work and how to make your own organization work a little better. In this chapter, I address some of the things that go wrong in organizations. This is something that managers don't like to talk about—the big publishing and consulting fortunes are built on "continuous improvement," "the search for excellence," or "total quality management," and the like. After all, what manager would want to be caught reading "How to Fix Your Pathological Company?"

The tendency to avoid thinking about problems is exacerbated by our culture. By temperament Americans are optimistic and positive. The impulse to attain the hallowed states of "optimal performance," "effectiveness," "world class," "best and brightest," "excellence," and other superlatives is strong—and, on balance, salutary. However, I suspect this tendency also often blinds us to what can go wrong. For instance, we have metaphors for "healthy" organizations (Bennis 1966) but not for sick ones. In the six decades or so that American academics and practitioners have sought first for organizational "efficiency," then "effectiveness," and finally "excellence," the study of incompetence and failure has rarely received more than passing attention. Only recently have the topics of "normal accidents" (Perrow 1984), "vicious circles" (Mausch 1985), and "organizational decline" (Whetten 1980) become somewhat fashionable. In the meantime, the damage done by serious organizational mistakes and failures has grown and grown.

The fact is, accidents do happen, even good companies mess up, and the natural state of organizations is dysfunction or death. Of the 600,000 or so businesses founded each year, over 90 percent do not reach their first birthday. Moreover, those organizations that are guaranteed survival by legislative or executive edict are widely known for their inefficiency, rigidity, unresponsiveness, and incompetence. For these reasons, I believe that the manager who is on guard against problems and admits and confronts them when they come up will win out in the long run.

Introducing Dysfunctions

Insofar as possible, this chapter uses the framework of Chapter 1 to identify some of the common maladies (or dysfunctions, as I call them) that are found in organizations. Much of what you read will be simple extensions of the logic of Chapter 1. Organizations experience some problems that the GBAS model does not deal with; and for these dysfunctions, I will have to introduce a few new but simple concepts. At the end of the chapter, I will illustrate the dysfunctions studied with an analysis of the failure of the Penn Central Railroad.

Most of the dysfunctions to be discussed stem from violations of the four facts of organizational life identified in the first chapter: fit, packages, opposites, and trade-offs. The first three disfunctions (frivolous complexity, loose boundaries, and impermeable boundaries) all occur when a component of the organization gets seriously out of fit with another. Although there are many types of misfit, the three about to be discussed seem to be the most common.

Dysfunction 1: Frivolous Complexity

Frivolous complexity takes place when an organization's activity system becomes more complex than is necessary for goal attainment. To understand frivolous complexity, think back to Backyard Enterprises in Chapter 1. Remember that the firm was effective because of its fine balance or fit between goal, boundaries, activity system, and the environment.

Just how tight this fit is becomes obvious if we consider what would happen to one component of the organization if any other component were to change. Imagine that our friend decides he is tired of driving the dusty back roads and would like to graduate to doing business in volume in the cities. He has essentially changed the portion of the environment to be addressed, and so his goals and ultimately his boundaries and activity system must now change radically.

Out of the Backyard, Into the Fire.   If his environmental focus broadens to include the larger towns, his domain gets much broader and more complex. Shops in town will want packaging, broader product offerings (leaf spring bushings for all models, not just the ones that break down the most), higher volume, transaction documents, monthly billing, constant quality levels, maybe even guarantees or credit. This in turn leads to greater complexity in the activity system, or less permeable boundaries, or some combination of both.

For instance, if a greater variety of models is to be offered, the activity system must add new features to accommodate the added variability in the production process—perhaps two production lines, or shift work. Also, if several different models are to be made, the lathe will have to be adjusted more frequently than every two weeks. This will require that the lathe operator be familiar with lathe setup and precision measurement, which of course results in less permeable boundaries, as these skills must now be possessed by lathe operators who come into the organization.

Alternatively, the owner could train the present lathe operator, in which case the greater complexity would be absorbed by adding a training function to the activity system rather than erecting higher boundaries. Note that if we don't make the boundaries less permeable, we will have to make the activity system more complex.

This type of trade-off arises again and again in organizations. If a university does not require incoming students to demonstrate proficiency in mathematics (a boundary), remedial math classes must be added to the curriculum (a more complex activity system). If an organization does not establish rigorous credit requirements (a less permeable boundary), it will require a collection function (another element in the activity system). If a restaurant wants to save money by buying live chickens (permeable entrance boundary), someone will have kill and dress them (more complex activity system).

The Backyard MBA. When trade-offs are not well managed, the organization usually ends up with something that it doesn't need or lacking something that it does need. Frivolous complexity involves things that are not needed. Consider one more "thought experiment" on our friend's factory. Let's suppose our friend goes to school and gets an MBA. Zealous in his newfound knowledge, he begins to "professionalize" his business. He institutes daily progress reports, carries out time and motion studies, prepares operational manuals, sets product standards, installs a timeclock and suggestion box, and starts a quality circle.

The result is obvious. He will need literate employees. He will spend his time at home managing instead of on the road visiting his geographically dispersed clients. His workers will be taken away from production by long meetings, training sessions, and paperwork. He will need middle managers. As boundaries become less permeable and the activity system more complex, costs will increase dramatically. Of course, his quality and person/ hour efficiency will improve, but who cares? These are improvements his environment does not care about. In other words, he has introduced administrative complexity unnecessary for goal attainment, hence the term frivolous complexity. Frivolous complexity is found in activity systems as a rule although frivolous impermeability also plagues boundaries.

The problem is not complexity in and of itself, but frivolous complexity. In a pharmaceutical company or refinery, for instance, all of the abovementioned mechanisms and more may be necessary. Or, if our friend were to change his goals to include a more diverse market, greater complexity would be necessary. In the present context, however, complexity in the activity system is increased without generating any real benefit.

Aside from increasing costs through unneeded overhead, frivolous complexity creates a number of other problems. It diverts attention away from the fundamental issues of goal attainment, and toward peripheral matters. This generates a distorted image of the firm's mission. It isolates management from contact with the environment, damaging customer relations and provoking unrealistic strategies. It distorts the value of organizational roles, inflates the importance of staff and management, and ignores the worker, the sales force, and product design, which in the final analysis are the heart of an organization.

Finally, frivolous complexity creates errors simply by virtue of its own weight. We know that the likelihood of error increases geometrically with the number of interrelated steps in a process (Aldrich 1978). Thus, each additional component in the activity system greatly increases the probability of error.

Of course, it is possible for organizations to be too simple. Often new organizations suffer because they have not yet developed basic systems and controls, and this is doubtless a cause of much organizational infant mortality—or "liability of newness," as the literature calls it. Excessive simplicity, however, is usually a temporary condition and can be resolved fairly quickly. Frivolous complexity, on the other hand, tends to be self-perpetuating and often very hard to change, probably because psychologically it is easy to establish rules and procedures and quite hard to give them up. Force of habit and reluctance to relinquish control seem to be major culprits.

Dysfunction 2: Impermeable Boundaries

Rigidity or impermeability in boundaries is analogous to frivolous complexity in the activity system. As organizations face the uncertainties of life, a common response is to erect ever-higher boundaries in an effort to block uncomfortable or noxious stimuli. Paul Hawken (1987) gives a classic example of the process at work in a retail businesses:

> Mrs. Green buys your widget and six months later returns it and wants her money back. New policy: "All goods must be returned within thirty days of purchase." Mr. Jones brings back your widget and says he bought it twenty days ago; he wants a refund. But you know that the discounter up the street just had a close out sale on the item, and you suspect that Jones might have bought the widget cheaply there and now wants a full refund from you. New

policy: "All items must be returned within thirty days and accompanied by the original receipt from this store." John Doe brings back one of your widgets and it looks as if it fell out of his car, or something equally serious. The widget is useless. New policy: "Damaged items will be exchanged only within thirty days of purchase, only if accompanied by original receipt from this store, and only if defect is a manufacturers defect." Mrs. White orders a widget and asks you to ship it to her home upstate. Three weeks later its returned to you in unrecognizable shape. The customer wants her money back but the trucker says she signed for it in "good condition" and he won't accept an insurance claim. New policy: "This merchandise left our store in first-class condition and shall not be returned for any reason without proper authorization. We definitely are not responsible for any damage whatsoever incurred at any time to any of our products while merchandise is in transit. Any merchandise returned to us will be refused. You must file a claim for damage, cost of repairs, shipping charges or replacement parts."

Hawken follows up his example with the following statement: "That's why so few North American companies have satisfactory customer relations. Management sees customers as an entity 'outside' the company, and this is especially true in the case of the big corporations and retailers. Businesses are armed to the teeth to prevent fraud, abuse, hassles, and ripoffs coming from customers or suppliers. They have elaborate procedures for dealing with anything that might go wrong in the area of service. Meanwhile, and not coincidentally, just about everything has gone wrong with American business" (192–193).

Couched in our own terms, in an effort to insulate themselves from negative environmental stimuli, these organizations erect rigid, highly impermeable boundaries which keep customers away and otherwise alienate stakeholders.

Not only are the boundaries that regulate material flows susceptible to impermeability. Rigid classification or coding systems may filter out essential information. IBM had no category for personal computers, except perhaps "toy" until the market became so large as to threaten its mini and mainframe businesses. Detroit similarly could not classify Japanese cars, except as toys, before significant markets were lost. The very architecture used for Apple's revolutionary Macintosh was discarded by Xerox as "esoteric." Polaroid's idea that a market might exist for an instantaneous photographic system was lost on Kodak until after Polaroid made millions as a competitor.

For organizations functioning in an uncertain or rapidly changing environment, impermeable boundaries are very dangerous, but even those in stable environments need some permeability. In addition to assuring contact with reality, permeable boundaries provide other benefits. Employees of organizations with impermeable boundaries tend to develop a sense of security or even smugness that comes from being artificially protected. They tend to perceive nonemployees as foreign at best, nuisances at worst. The purpose of organizational activities also becomes unclear to those who are excessively buffered from the environment, resulting in errors and inefficiencies. By admitting a very limited range of people, things, and ideas into the organization, impermeable boundaries reduce variability inside the organization, leading to a sameness—almost a numbness—throughout. This sameness suppresses creativity and is a real liability in times of crisis or change.

Dysfunction 3: Loose Boundaries

As is the case with frivolous complexity, organizations seem to be more prone to excessively impermeable rather than overly permeable boundaries, but the malady does exist. Public and volunteer organizations often have boundaries that are too loose. The enrollment economy of public universities is a good example. Legislatures apportion money to schools according to the number of student-hours taught. Schools in turn admit totally unqualified students in order to boost budgets. By loosening entrance boundaries, the mediocrity of academic programs is ensured, and huge variability in student quality is introduced. To accommodate this variability, remedial courses and other services, such as increased counseling staff, must be provided. This requires a more complex activity system, which in turn reduces efficiency and diverts attention from the organizational goal of higher education.

Both the Boy Scouts and the LDS (Mormon) church have had similar difficulties. Some years back, the Boy Scouts experienced serious problems because of availability, federal formula funding to increase Scouting rolls, and overemphasis on growth (i.e., insufficient linkage between goals and the environment). During year end drives, dues were reduced to ten cents per month (a significant loosening of entrance boundaries), and thousands enrolled only to drop out subsequently. Large numbers of inner-city youths were enrolled without their knowledge to take advantage of federal monies available to pay the dues for disadvantaged groups.

In theory, this should have occasioned a tremendous overload for the volunteer adults that serve as Scout leaders. In practice, the activity system was only slightly affected because the new Scouts existed only on paper. In the LDS case, however, loose boundaries often overtax the activity system. Evangelistic fervor and ease of entry (converts may be admitted with as little as one visit to church and a week of missionary lessons) produce a large, heterogeneous influx of converts. Many do not catch on to the rigorous spiritual and moral discipline of the church and soon become inactive. Because of the LDS commitment to reach every member monthly with a personal visit at home, active members spend considerable time visiting inactives. To this visiting time, add the time needed for various church responsibilities (the church has no paid ministry) and the domestic concerns of traditionally large Mormon families. The resulting overload often affects the quality of church programs and creates stress in active families.

Dysfunction 4: Goal Fixation

Although an organization may carefully select its domain or turf to maximize fit between what the environment needs and what the organization has to offer, no organization is ever free from competing demands. Even Rolls Royce, I'm sure, has occasional concerns about price, as does Beatrice about unrelated diversification. For less unique organizations, competing goals are very frequent. Lower prices mean greater market share but slimmer profit margins. Increased research and development expenditures mean greater adaptability but higher costs. Cost cutting promotes efficiency but invariably makes someone unhappy. In addition to striking a balance between the components of the organization, managers need to strike a balance between incompatible demands that come from both the inside and the outside. In some cases this is fairly easy. A rock quarry, for instance, will clearly be more interested in cost containment than in product innovation. Similarly, a prison will be more concerned with security than with friendly service. But in all organizations, some kind of prioritization must be effected.

Unfortunately, in most collectives, and in many individuals, there is a tendency to reject the ambiguity inherent in (Miller 1993; Pauchant and Mitroff 1992) balancing contradictory demands. It is easy to mobilize people around one dominant idea like "Quality is job one." It is much harder to deal with "Quality is job one, but market studies show that if our costs don't come down by 15 percent our current customers will buy a Hundai rather than a Ford."

It is also true that some goals are inherently much more attractive than others. Quality is easier to sell to the troops than cost reduction. Similarly, growth is a much more appealing goal than reliability. The rewards for growth come in the form of more resources, greater promotion opportunities, and more status, all of which are much more tangible and appealing than the stability and continuity that come from reliability.

Often a person, a top management cadre, or an entire industry will have a predisposition toward certain goals (Perrow 1971). Hitler was hell-bent on expansion, as are a host of megalomaniac CEOs. Nixon was obsessed with security. The fashion industries are fixated on change. Whether a given predisposition makes sense or not of course depends on how well it fits the requirements of the general environment. However, no matter how appropriate an obsession is, it still has the capability of crowding out other matters of importance. When an organization reaches the point where only behaviors supporting one kind of goal are acknowledged and rewarded, goal fixation has occurred.

Goal fixation always leads to impairment, because organizations need to accomplish more than one task to survive over time. Chris Argyris (1964) suggests that all organizations must attain at least threshold levels of three attributes: efficiency, harmony, and flexibility. At the same time that these factors are necessary, they are also incompatible (March 1991). The experimentation needed to be flexible generates waste and reduces efficiency. Specialization is efficient because it enables people to become proficient in a limited sphere of competence with minimal training, but it alienates people from one another and creates disparate perspectives, resulting in disharmony. Flexibility implies change and adjustment, which will invariably upset someone, thus eroding harmony.

Hence, the successful organization must simultaneously maintain at least a modicum of efficiency, harmony, and flexibility, while accentuating those factors that are most appropriate given the nature of the environment. The research organization that becomes fixated on creativity and innovation (i.e., flexibility) is likely to fail as internal conflict (disharmony) is left to rage out of control, and reckless use of available resources (inefficiency) eventually impedes the discovery of new knowledge. The factory that becomes fixated on cost containment (efficiency) at the expense of harmony and flexibility will be left vulnerable to strikes and sabotage and will be rendered unable to carry out even minor changes in product or delivery.

Activity System Failures:
Dysfunctions in Structures and Flows

Although many problems in organizations have their origin in imbalances between goals, boundaries, activity systems, or other components, there are dysfunctions that affect elements of the organization separately, without necessarily causing imbalances between them. Dysfunctions in two critical dimensions of the activity system, structures and flows, can cause considerable grief in their own right. Structures are standards or patterns of interaction and exchange that guide and control organizational activities. Aside from the formal hierarchy or organization chart, structures include informal patterns of communication or influence, standards of all kinds, and systems used to channel the movement of ideas, things, or people through the organization. Flows are the actual exchanges or transactions that flow through structures. They include information, affect, physical resources, formal or informal decisions, authorizations, requests, and commands. The difference between these two should become clearer as we progress.

There are numerous structural dysfunctions, some of them widely known and easily detected, some harder to find. Overcentralization, the concentration of decision-making powers in few individuals or departments, is so common as to require little comment. Overcentralization overloads the top of the organization, slows down virtually all flows, underutilizes the firm's human resources, and provokes strategic and tactical errors because decisions are made far from the people closest to the issues under consideration (Kets de Vries and Miller 1984).

Frequently overcentralization provokes other dysfunctions. This is the case with bypassing, which is often caused by overcentralization. In overcentralized organizations, there is a great temptation to go around or bypass formal hierarchical channels in order to gain direct access to decision-makers. Taken to its extreme, bypassing renders whole portions of the organization impotent by ignoring their existence. This in turn may lead to formalism, a very common structural failure which belongs to a family of dysfunctions I call dualisms.

Dysfunction 5: Formalism—The Most Common Dualism

Dualisms are unplanned or unnecessary redundancies in the organization. Some dual structures are deliberate. Matrix structures, for instance, contain dual hierarchies by design. Most redundancies, however, are accidental and arise from distortions in the organization. In the case of bypassing, the bypasser secures approval for a given course of action informally by appealing directly to the top of the organization, then sends a formal request "up through channels." This creates the impression that intermediate organizational levels serve some real function when, in fact, bypassing has robbed the middle levels of their function, and the formal use of channels is merely a gloss to hide the real status quo. When organizations provide legitimacy and resources for formal structures and procedures that are not used by large numbers of their employees or clients, formalisms exist. Formalisms are probably the most prevalent of dualisms.

Structural formalisms are most common, but formalisms can also be found in boundaries and goals. Selection processes often contain formalisms, so much so that research on job search behavior reveals that people who use formal application procedures rather than personal contacts in seeking employment land lower-paying jobs and experience less job satisfaction. Granovetter (1973) tells of one job candidate who received a formal letter of rejection from an institution after he had already secured a job there using his informal contacts. Formalisms exist at other entry boundaries such as contract bidding and related screening processes.

Once after trying in vain to get through the security clearance procedures of my local phone company, I was informed by an employee that all I really needed to do was bang on the heavy steel door and yell "Coke man." Similar secret codes are rife at organizational boundaries. Organizations also frequently have formal goals and "real" goals (Selznick 1966). (As I mentioned earlier, real goals are most easily inferred from actual behaviors rather than from formal statements.)

Formalisms in accounting systems are a hallmark of failing organizations, Rolls Royce and the Penn Central being the two most celebrated examples. In the last years before its collapse, Rolls Royce accountants capitalized research and development expenditures in order to show a paper profit and credited income from engine sales they expected to make (Argenti, 1976). This formalism extended to board meetings, where each director received a red and a green folder. Argenti explains: "The green folder contained all the important matters to be discussed and was compulsory reading for all directors. All the financial data—masses of it in great detail—were in the red folder, i.e., the voluntary one, which few of the directors would have time to absorb" (91). Formalisms in Penn Central accounting will be covered later on, but one telling example was the crediting of real estate sales that were to be paid for over ten- and fifteen-year periods as current income.

Although some gap between the real and the ideal is unavoidable in all organizations, formalisms almost always cause damage, and a serious formalism can canker the entire organization. Formalistic organizations are never fully efficient because they must simultaneously maintain two disparate systems. They commit many errors because of confusion about which system is being used or referred to in a given instance. Clients or other external stakeholders have particularly bitter experiences with formalistic organizations because, from their position on the outside, they can sense the existence of formalisms: but they cannot easily identify where the two systems diverge, nor discern which mechanisms produce results and which lead nowhere.

Formalistic organizations generate high turnover for the same reason. New employees quickly become frustrated at trying to secondguess the system and leave. Finally, the climate of a formalistic organization is always distrustful, because dishonesty and deception are an unavoidable concomitant of dualism.

Dysfunction 6: Factionalism

Formalistic structures are essentially parallel; two different channels are used to obtain the same result or deal with the same subject matter. Factional structures, the fruit of another dualism, are oppositional. That is to say, while formalistic structures or procedures fulfill the same function, they generally do not compete. Rather, one structure is "real" and takes precedence over the formal or "phony" structure. Often they are somewhat coordinated to preserve an appearance of integrity, as in the case of bypassing mentioned above. Another example would be the firm that keeps two sets of books; the two mechanisms address the same subject matter and are coordinated, except that different people see different information.

Factional structures, on the other hand, are always isolated from one another and often oppose each other. Frequently they follow the contours of the division of labor and contain their own hierarchies (Lauman and Pappi 1976). Factional structures in an organization do not always develop into factionalism and overt conflict, but the existence of self-contained departmental or functional "islands" without ties to other groups is always potentially divisive, and the move from latent to overt conflict seldom comes at an opportune moment.

Crises are known to push apart factional structures into fullblown warring factions, but sudden prosperity can have the same effect by raising questions about the distribution of excess resources. Even when factional structures do not provoke conflict, they degrade the quality of communication and coordination in the organization and slow organizational flows. Ironically, factionalism may reduce formalism, because factions are quick to point out the inconsistencies of the other party.

Dysfunction 7: Polarization

Factional strife may evolve into polarization, a serious, debilitating dysfunction. Polarization exists when there are only two categories for stimuli in the organization—good or bad, in or out, high or low, friend or foe. All ideas, proposals, decisions, and people *must* be classified. Nothing is held in abeyance, no one may sit on the fence, nothing is ambiguous. Everything passes through the same coarse filter of the faction's ideology or interests. When an organization becomes highly polarized, the factions on either side of an issue are incapable of dialogue or compromise. The only way of resolving differences is through unlimited conflict which renders one pole utterly defeated and the other totally dominant. If the losers are not forced out of the organization, they are reduced to sullen passivity.

This of course hinders coordination and saps motivation, but the greatest damage of polarization comes from the perceptual distortions it provokes (Bozeman and Slusher 1979). Because reality is made up of many, many different stimuli that can be categorized and recategorized in myriad ways, the incidence of polarization freezes the organization into an unreal categorization system, one that is woefully oversimplified relative to reality both inside and outside the organization. Moreover, the pervasive effects of polarization keep the organization from developing new and more accurate ways of looking at things, because any innovation will quickly be pushed into one of the two polar categories or rejected as subversive and disloyal (Cameron et al. 1987).

Things get worse after one of the poles has been defeated, because all dissension is eliminated—and with it any hope of organizational objectivity. Moderates, who are treated badly as polarization gets underway, are now totally discredited as traitors to a winning cause, and only a small group of radicalized or opportunistic fanatics retain any influence.

Although factionalism often leads to polarization, other causes exist. Demographic, ethnic, or other discontinuities in the composition of the organization can provoke polarization with or without observable factions. The United States is gradually becoming polarized as the distribution of wealth becomes more and more divided between a wealthy class of professionals, executives, and entrepreneurs, and an underclass of welfare recipients and semiliterate, unskilled workers. These same divisions intrude into many American organizations. Most developing countries have experienced similar bimodal distributions of wealth and education throughout their histories.

When systems contain such sharply bimodal distributions, polarization can be set off by all manner of trivial causes because the composition of the organization favors binary categories (see Bossevain 1974 and Hawkins 1984 for anthropological examples). The same holds true for factionalism, and to a much lesser degree, for formalism: the existence of two dominant categories in an organization provokes oppositional or two-faced structures.

The Terrible Twos: Oppositional Pairs. Even without bimodalism in the composition of the organization, there is a natural tendency for systems to polarize. The existence of "reciprocal opposition" as a central feature of human systems has been observed in the classical writings of most branches of the behavioral sciences including linguistics (Roman), psychology (Piaget), sociology (Simmel), and anthropology (Levi Strauss). Most of this work identifies the oppositional pair—two mutually exclusive and contrasting categories—as the starting point for the development of mental schema, symbolic systems, and social structures (Levi Strauss 1963; Saussure 1959). As systems mature, they gradually develop more numerous and subtle categories which come progressively closer to adequately explaining the great variance and subtlety that exists in nature.

However, because binary classification is such a fundamental and primitive aspect of human cognition, there is an ever-present tendency to regress back to polarized categories, especially under stress or strong emotion. For this reason, the management of variance—mostly accomplished through the management of boundaries—is one of the great challenges faced in organizations. If excessive variance is allowed, the organization may never develop a coherent identity or culture. If boundaries are uneven and bimodal variance obtains, or if competing groups are allowed to mobilize into successively fewer coalitions, factionalism and polarization may result (Dahrendorf 1959). If, on the other hand, too little variance is permitted, the organization will be too homogeneous to understand the environment and adapt to change, just as in an organization where polarization has led to the suppression of dissent and to an artificial homogeneity.

Dysfunction 8: Blocked Flows

Dysfunctions in flows are quite common in organizations but are less apparent than structural dysfunctions. The most dramatic dysfunctions are blocked flows. Like a plugged fuel line or toilet, a blocked flow occurs any time ideas, things, or people get held up at some point in the system. Faulty organization structures may create bottlenecks that limit flows, but the actual blockage usually comes from a failure in some component of the structure rather than the overall design of the organization itself. In fact, almost all outright blockages are intentional acts of individuals or groups. Strikes and deliberate sabotage are typical examples, but more subtle manifestations are refusal to provide routine signatures or grant routine requests. The effect of a blocked flow is usually so debilitating that immediate remedies are applied or disaster follows.

Because the effects are so dramatic, there is little need to be concerned about the diagnosis of blocked flows. Rather, the existence of a blockage should be exploited for its diagnostic value. The location of blockages provides insights into activity system flaws or impermeability of boundaries. The frequency of blockages and the way they are removed provide important information about the organization's ability to process information and adapt to crises. Moreover, the general discomfort provided by blockages may generate the needed resolve for reforms that would be put off under less pressing circumstances. Happy is the organization that experiences blockages before its adaptive capacity has been diminished by other dysfunctions.

Dysfunction 9: Irrelevant Content

Irrelevant content in flows is an undramatic but insidious dysfunction that afflicts most organizations. Irrelevant content occurs when a flow (message, request, decision, permission, statement of affect, attempt at influence, etc.) contains an unnecessary element. Obvious examples abound, but not all irrelevant content is easily identified. A promotion based on friendship rather than competence contains irrelevant content. Most sexual harassment involves irrelevant content. Requests for information or suggestions that contain implicit guidance about what kind of feedback is desired are a common form of irrelevant content.

The values or "culture" that organizations (often unwittingly) transmit to employees may contain excess content that is irrelevant or inimical to performance. As an example, in one large American corporation there was a general image of the effective sales person as extroverted, jovial, and dominant. This stereotype had found its way into selection and socialization patterns and was never challenged until an empirical study of the personal characteristics of effective sales staff revealed these tendencies to be totally unrelated to performance.

Politicization is the major source of irrelevant content. It is defined here as a preoccupation with the distribution of power and resources within the organization rather than their generation. This preoccupation causes all manner of irrelevant content to be added to organizational flows. Friendships are formed for their value in securing resources. Information is transmitted or withheld on the basis of its value for influencing resource distribution. Decisions are based on distributional rather than technical criteria, and so on.

Politicization adds all manner of arbitrary symbolic content to flows, for when organizations divorce the accumulation of resources from their generation, productive activity is immediately curtailed, and energy is diverted to the manipulation of symbols. In other words, if the distribution of rewards is not closely linked to people's production, some other means of distribution must be worked out. And this means of distribution will involve complex manipulation of symbols so as to avoid the obvious solution of tying rewards to production. This feeds what I call the BS principle: the more time you spend learning to look like you deserve rewards (i.e., the manipulation of symbols), the less time you have to actually deserve them (i.e., the less time you have for production).

As the members of the organization develop impressive but arbitrary symbols justifying preferential access to dwindling resources (which are dwindling because symbolic activity has replaced productive activity), much time and energy will be spent in conflict over whose arbitrary symbols are best. The winner in this conflict will usually be the coalition that promises to distribute rewards most broadly. However, conditions of declining productivity and general distribution diminish rewards per person to the level of insignificance, so that a coalition favoring narrower distribution of rewards will arise. (In the meantime, productive people leave for organizations where productivity is rewarded, diminishing productive capacity still more.) This in turn leads to or exacerbates the polarization and factionalization discussed above.

Just as impermeable boundaries distort inputs from the environment, irrelevant content distorts internal communication, burdens relationships with extra baggage, and slows down organizational processes. The interpretation of messages becomes problematic because of their extra content, and energies are spent in nonproductive activities. Irrelevant flows are not immediately destructive, but their parasitic effects eventually drag the organization down to impotence.

An industrywide example of irrelevant content helps explain the dismal performance of the British coal industry between World Wars I and II. Continental and even Scottish mines during the interwar period had generally higher profitability and lower costs than British mines at the time. Several explanations have been offered, including a generous minimum wage law, poor coal seams, and small scale, atomistic production, but a recent study (Dittenfass 1988) identifies several British firms that did very well under these constraints and attributes low performance to poor management.

The study attributes poor performance to "entrepreneurial failure" and suggests that the network of contacts which connected British coal firms contained mostly irrelevant content: "These interlocking interests do not necessarily indicate any unification of policy, but have grown up historically as a result of family and personal ownership or investment rather than in any attempt to secure economies through the association of neighboring or competing concerns." Hence, the coal companies had a structure which could have diffused new technologies and business practices, but this structure was dominated by irrelevant factors which impeded the flow of useful content from one economic unit to another.

Dysfunction 10: Low Density

Flows may be blocked or corrupted with irrelevant content, but sometimes flows are of insufficient volume to begin with, or become drastically reduced through structural deficiencies or conflict. I use the term "low density" or insufficient density to describe this state. I see it all the time in student project groups. At the beginning of the semester I assign a group paper and preside over some kind of formal process to bring students together. As the semester progresses, some groups will approach me to clarify the assignment, complain about individual members, or ask for advice.

Invariably, however, I am besieged on the eve of the due date by individuals with whom I have had no previous contact. Moreover, I usually learn that they have had almost no contact with their colleagues. They always come as individuals or at most as pairs (never as a group) to inform me that no one will cooperate, no paper has been written, and that yes, they will throw something together, but they'll have to do all the work themselves.

Upon inquiry, I discover that the "group" simply never generated enough flows to get anything done. Few meetings were held, few messages were exchanged in or outside of meetings, few opinions were expressed, few decisions were attempted, no arguments ensued, no frivolity was enjoyed—nothing. Because any collective effort must attain a threshold of interaction between individuals before productive activity can take place, these groups never produced anything.

The same phenomenon, and its opposite, can be found in organizations, sometimes with disastrous results. In Hadley's (1986) description of the fumbled U.S. attempt to free the Iranian hostages, he repeatedly shows how lack of interaction between the diverse individuals and groups who composed (better, who never really did compose) the Delta Force, led to error upon error and finally to disaster. The following quote is typical:

> Night operations have a deserved reputation for difficulty. Even when they have been meticulously rehearsed by men who trust one another and have fought together, things tend to go wrong. On that twenty-fourth of April, 1980, at this lonely stretch of desert, code-named Desert One, some of the units and men about to come together had not even seen one another before. Other units in the mission profoundly distrusted one another. Nine different groups of men had to meld together in the hostile dark, harassed by constant noise and sand blown from the aircraft engines, which were deliberately left running all night for immediate takeoff.
>
> There was Delta Force itself, the ninety-three commandoes who were to perform the main mission of rescuing the hostages from the U.S. embassy. There was a thirteen-man Army Ranger detachment from Europe, who were going to free the four American hostages held separately from the others in the Iranian Foreign Ministry. These men had barely met other parts of the rescue force. There were some dozen Army antiaircraft experts with Redeye antiaircraft missiles. There were eleven men fluent in Farsi, who were going to drive the trucks in the final attack phase of the operation . . . they had rehearsed with other parts of the force for only a few weeks. (4–5)

It is no wonder that Delta Force never made it to Tehran. Had they been students of mine, they wouldn't have turned in their project, either.

Dysfunction in Action: The Demise of the Penn Central

On June 21, 1970, the United States' largest private corporation filed for bankruptcy after losing approximately one million dollars a day for the length of its 871-day history. The Penn Central originated in early 1968 from a friendly merger of the New York Central and the Pennsylvania Railroads, then the two largest in the nation. Although both roads were doing poorly at the time of their merger, the New York Central had experienced a recent turnaround, and the Pennsy had once been commonly acclaimed as the world's best-run railroad (Chandler 1977). An analysis of the short history of this ill-fated behemoth provides examples of almost all of the dysfunctions described up to this point. (Most of my information comes from Binzen and Daughen's excellent book, *The Wreck of the Penn Central*.)

The diverse history of the two roads created a mixed type organization from the outset of the merger. Even the two companies' colors, red and green, were complementary opposites, a symbolism invariably associated with oppositional pairs (Bossevain 1974; Levi Strauss 1963). The Central arose out of the amalgamation of ten smaller railroads and their takeover by the notorious Cornelius Vanderbilt with the aid of ruthless speculative maneuver. The Central never lost its taste for aggressive and flexible, if sometimes erratic, moves. Its structure was highly centralized, its management individualistic with a quantitative bent.

In contrast, the Pennsylvania Railroad was founded by a group of civic-minded business and government leaders concerned not with speculation but economic development. In general it grew through internal expansion rather than acquisition. Career managers dominated its management from the beginning. They were generally sociable, conservative team players who had come up through the ranks. The Pennsy was a marvel of painstaking, meticulous organization which had been perfected over two generations as one of the world's largest railroads.

These separate tendencies may have been exacerbated as the two neighboring railroads competed. As we noted in Chapter 1, it is common in competitive relationships for parties to differentiate as a means of exploiting each other's weaknesses. (Remember how early in the burger wars McDonald's locked up the family market by appealing to young children and their parents, so Burger King had to target single young adults?) GM has traditionally stressed styling and innovation while Ford stressed quality, and so on. In any case, the merger brought together two very different institutions. This quote from Binzen and Daughen (1971) is exemplary:

> James Sykes to the contrary, the PRR and Central were not like "two peas in a pod." In operating style, in marketing philosophy, in personnel, they differed sharply. The Pennsylvania, stolid, steady and traditional, carried ore over mountains. It was "volume oriented," and its operations were highly decentralized. It generally promoted from within its own ranks. The Central was smaller, scrappier, hungrier, and more inclined to abandon the book and innovate. Pearlman once said: "After you've done a thing the same way for two years, look it over carefully. After five years, look at it with suspicion. After ten years, throw it away and start all over again." (70)

Despite an organization chart that balanced Pennsy and Central people fairly well, and despite optimistic public affirmations to the contrary, there was constant friction between the two groups, which probably did not polarize completely only because the organization deteriorated so quickly that not even the oppositional pairs remained intact, and because the finance department of the Pennsylvania contained a faction estranged from both the Central management and from the rest of the Pennsylvania management.

Quoting Binzen and Daughen (1971) again,

> Not one of these operational problems was insuperable. But the problem of incompatible executives proved to be just that. "The most difficult part of the merger," William A. Lashlen, Penn Central's perceptive vice president for public relations and advertising, said in an interview nine months before the bankruptcy, "is the human personality. You can combine tracks and stations but getting people together is something else." Another executive said it was "human nature" for the reds and greens to fight it out. "Not that you'll find blood an inch thick on the floor. It's all been fairly gentlemanly. But I don't see the rivalry as having lessened at all lately. It's surprisingly deep rooted in the human psyche." And he was talking at a point seventeen months after the merger began. (71)

These divisions were causing conflicts and impeding coordination and decisionmaking up till the end.

Rather than combatting institutional differences by building a cohesive top management team, the top executives of the new railroad entertained a very low density of contacts. The president, Alfred E. Pearlman, did not even live in the state where the railroad was headquartered:

> Pearlman was president of the New York Central, and at one minute after midnight, he would become president of the merged Penn Central. He had been a reluctant partner in the marriage of the two giants. His mistrust of his colleagues on the Pennsylvania was no secret. He was comfortable in the New York Central's boardroom on the thirty-second floor of 230 Park Avenue in Manhattan. The new Penn Central board room on the eighteenth floor of Six Penn Center in Philadelphia, the old Pennsylvania board room, was in the wrong city and belonged to the wrong railroad. The railroad he was supposed to run would be headquartered in Philadelphia, but Perlman had long since decided that he would continue to live in Larchmont, New York, and would work out of Park Avenue. (Binzen and Daughen 1971: 2)

The CEO, Stuart T. Saunders, spent most of his time cultivating his external network, cutting into the time and energy that could have been used to weld together the two foreign bodies. He belonged to all the important clubs in Philadelphia, maintained an impressive array of Washington contacts, and participated in several civic organizations and corporate boards:

With all of that, Saunders somehow found time for outside directorships—U.S. Steel, Chase Manhattan Bank, Bell Telephone Company of Pennsylvania, First Pennsylvania Banking and Trust Company, among many others—and for corporate good works. He served on the high-level Business Council, the John F. Kennedy Library Corporation, and the Philadelphia Bicentennial Commission. He advised President Lyndon B. Johnson on labor–management policy. He was vice chairman of the National Coal Policy Conference and Philadelphia metropolitan area chairman of the National Alliance of Businessmen. He was also chairman of the board of trustees at his alma mater, Roanoke College in Virginia. (Binzen and Daughen 1971: 96)

The third member of the Penn Central triumvirate, David Bevan, as we will learn later, had always been isolated organizationally and was snubbed by an unnecessary demotion incident to the merger. The working relationship between the three was so superficial that after the Penn Central failed, they gave totally contradictory accounts of their roles in the organization. Testifying before the Senate Commerce Committee, Saunders said of Pearlman's operating authority: "When Mr. Perlman was president, he was in charge of railroad operations and he had full authority. He may not agree completely with this, but he was given complete responsibility" (Binzen and Daughen 1971: 110).

In contrast, Robert Bedingfeld, a respected authority on transportation writing for the *New York Times,* observed, "Not only did many Pennsylvania-trained operating employees belittle many of Perlman's ideas so long as their overall 'chief' was their old boss, but also Mr. Saunders turned his attention more to an aggressive diversification program than to reviewing Mr. Perlman's suggestions for spending large sums to upgrade the consolidated company's transportation plant and expanding the railroad's marketing activities" (Binzen and Daughen 1971: 89).

Fortune magazine suggested that Perlman had no budgetary authority, and that Bevan jealously controlled the company's purse strings: "Although Perlman made up his budgets, the outlays and other key financial data were controlled by Bevan, who was suspected of favoring land investments over the railroad." *Modern Railroad* made similar comments: "Again, every one who knows Al Perlman's ability concedes that if he had been permitted to run the property instead of being frustrated at every turn, it might not have wound up the biggest bankruptcy in U.S. corporate history" (Binzen and Daughen 1971: 88).

In contrast, Bevan assigns all authority to Pearlman, minimal intervention to Saunders, and no clout to himself: "Saunders said, 'As soon as the merger takes place, I'll be the boss.' But he never exercised authority. He seemed to be afraid of Perlman. Some of us thought he wanted to be in a position to say, 'I'm not an operating man,' if anything went wrong. . . . I had no control over expenditures. At every board meeting, I said, 'Cash is tight, we've stretched this rubber band as far as it will stretch'" (Binzen and Daughen 1971: 110).

The side-by-side existence of remnants of two corporate systems with only low-density contacts connecting top management stimulated dualisms and led to an excessively complex activity system which multiplied errors: "In railroad freight handling, the trick is to collect as quickly as possible all of the boxcars that are going to the same place and get them rolling over the rails. If an entire train of freight cars loaded with shipments to the same destination can be assembled, that's wonderful. It means the train can run past all intermediate classification yards to the final delivery point. More often, blocks of cars must be left off at specific points for rerouting. Under the best of conditions, this is time consuming. It requires careful classification of cars so that yard dispatchers know what is to go where" (Binzen and Daughen 1971: 117). Because the Pennsylvania and Central served many of the same cities, a major advantage of the merger should have been simplification of operations and economies of scale.

However, because the activity systems were combined early but never streamlined to reduce the total number of classifications nor harmonized to provide common terminology, severe operational errors proliferated:

When the PRR and Central merged, the freight classification system went pfutt. Thousands of employees didn't know the new system; the dispatchers for connecting railroads didn't know it; shippers didn't know it. Cars piled up at yards where they weren't expected or wanted. Cars got separated from waybills—the papers supposedly accompanying them giving routes and destinations. Harassed yard superintendents sent out whole trains of no-waybill cars just to get rid of them. Full freight trains sat idle on main-line tracks, delaying other shipments and creating shortages of yard locomotives needed to move them. In one case, a coal train of more than 100 cars was said to have been lost for ten days outside Syracuse.

Confusion was greatest in such cities as Chicago, Cincinnati, and Cleveland, where the PRR and Central both had freight yards. In Chicago, for example, the Pennsylvania yard was at 59th Street and the Central yard at nearby Elkhart, Indiana. When the merger began, Penn Central asked shippers whose freight was to be routed through 59th Street to show "PCP" (Penn Central-Pennsylvania) on their waybills. Those using Elkhart were to show "PCN" (Penn Central-New York Central). "Time went by," explained a Penn Central executive, "and shippers began routing just 'PC'. Suddenly, we discovered a flood of misdirected cars. Cars were going to 59th Street and their waybills to Elkhart. Congestion grew. And as the cars moved to Columbus or Fort Wayne, the problems moved with them. Soon it was all over the map."

A good computer system might have helped untangle the mess of freight cars strung out all over, but Penn Central's computer system wasn't any good—not at this point. That was because there were two systems. Each road used a different method of generating freight-car movement information—the basis for car tracings. Both had used IBM computers to record freight movements, but while the PRR fed printouts and punched tapes to its computers the Central used IBM punch cards. The PRR used a Teletype inquiry system, the Central a cathode-ray TV setup. Like virtually everything else on the two railroads, the computers also differed. The Central's "random access disc file" updated car information quickly. The PRR's, though a disc file, was not "random access" and it updated information only periodically. (Binzen and Daughen 1971: 117–118)

The complexity of the activity system is further revealed by this quote:

A railroad functions best when it can assemble unit trains (where all cars are bound for the same destination) for long haul trips. Under these conditions, operating costs are lower, and there are fewer delays and fewer misrouted shipments. If, at the final destination, there are loop tracks leading to the terminal, so much the better. Loop tracks enable the train to leave the main line and approach a terminal to unload cars, then reenter the main line. This eliminates the costly and time-consuming process of stopping the train, uncoupling the car or cars to be unloaded, then switching them onto the spur leading to the terminal or dock. This kind of an operation provides high utilization of equipment and manpower, matters of efficiency that all railroads strive for.

The Penn Central, when it opened for business, did not have this type of operation. It was a "yard heavy" railroad, burdened with an overabundance of terminals. While there were many long-haul and unit shipments among its 1,720 daily freight trains, the Penn Central, proportionately, operated far more trains made up of individual carloads than any other railroad. This type of train is the most expensive to assemble. It requires the efforts of dozens of yard crews to bring the cars to be shipped to various connecting points. These crews use yard equipment to do the job, equipment that demands heavy power, which is also expensive. Moving the cars is a slow process, and classifying the cars at the connecting points for shipment to the final destination is just as slow.

Once at the destination, the same costly, time-consuming process must be reversed. The train must be broken down, the individual cars assigned to yard crews, who then transport them to the owner's docks or terminals.

The inefficiency connected with this type of an operation was something the Penn Central never overcame. The railroad spent more than fifteen cents out of every freight revenue dollar it received for yard transportation expenses. On other railroads, the average yard transportation expense was less than ten cents on a dollar. This difference cost the Penn Central about $80 million a year. (Binzen and Daughen 1971: 117)

As if operating problems were not enough, serious factionalism and a historic flaw in railroads' division of labor provoked financial problems. Traditionally, railroads have isolated the finance function from the rest of the organization. As a result, operating executives have tended not to critically analyze or fine tune capital allocations and their distribution among the various functions, while finance personnel have emphasized the manipulation and management of money without critically analyzing budgetary needs.

This tendency was severely exacerbated on the Penn Central by the formation of a finance faction around disgruntled vice president David Bevan. Bevan was removed from the board of directors when the companies merged and had been passed over for promotion earlier, leaving him bitter and resentful. He remained with the company only as a personal favor to board member Richard Mellon. Even before the merger, however, Bevan had been aloof from the rest of the organization. One executive stated: "It was common talk before the merger . . . that there were two Pennsylvania Railroads. There was Bevan's railroad and there was our railroad. Bevan wouldn't let his men talk to officers of other departments" (Binzen and Daughen 1971: 84).

This factionalism had two main effects. First, there was constant conflict about money, the operational side of the firm wanting to spend and the financial side wanting to save, and no mechanisms were devised for rationally deciding what expenses could be borne and what projects must be sacrificed. In the absence of a viable channel to resolve these differences, budget politicking grew. Because the operational side, which contained the CEO, was stronger than Bevan's finance feud, spending was excessive. This led inexorably to cash flow problems and excessive borrowing, which ultimately caused bankruptcy.

Second, there was little monitoring of the activities of finance, just the constant pressure for more money. In the absence of controls from the board or CEO, irregularities in the finance function multiplied, and the entrance boundaries for capital became lower and lower. The first shortfalls were covered by bank loans supported by collateral and subject to standard banking practices. As matters got worse, the company issued bonds, which required review by the Securities and Exchange Commission but did not have the same guarantees as bank loans. As the Penn Central's liquidity worsened, the railroad began issuing commercial paper—essentially interest-bearing IOUs with no guarantees whatever.

Other boundaries were as loose as or looser than boundaries for the entrance of capital. In slightly more than two years of existence, the Penn Central spent over $1.6 billion. When it went bankrupt on June 21, 1970, it had a little over seven million dollars in the bank. Several faulty boundary-maintaining mechanisms let cash hemorrhage out. Billing was very slow. A government official investigating in the aftermath of the bankruptcy found the company excessively lenient in its handling of accounts receivable: "The ICC requires that all railroad invoices be paid by shippers within seven working days. We went over their books and found they had twenty-eight days of receivables, four times what they should have. Based on a year's revenues, this amounts to $150 million in cash owed to them that they were letting sit idle at one time. They weren't billing properly" (Binzen and Daughen 1971: 281).

In order to gain union support for the merger, Saunders agreed that attrition be used as the only mechanism for personnel reductions. Given the considerable duplication of resources created by the merger, this represented a considerable waste of scarce resources; payment for unnecessary employees was estimated at around $120 million yearly. Executive salaries were high for a cash-starved railroad. Even on the day of bankruptcy, the board approved several raises for individual managers. Further, the Penn Central made several outside investments that showed very little concern for where the money was going.

Much of this faulty boundary keeping was facilitated by formalism tolerated in financial management. Creative accounting measures were employed to maximize income formally so the extent of the financial difficulties would be known only to insiders. One employee even received a raise in recognition of his income manipulating skills: "William S. Cook, vice president and comptroller, wrote a note to Bevan marked 'personal and confidential' on October 5, 1967. In the note, Cook requested that the salary of Charles S. Hill, manager of general accounting, be raised from $25,500 to $27,500. As justification, Cook said: 'His imaginative accounting is adding millions of dollars annually to our reported income.'" The ICC's bureau of accounts concluded: "In general the management of merged Penn Central adopted the former Pennsylvania Railroad's policy of maximizing income. The result was an increase in income without a corresponding increase in cash flow, thus obscuring the carrier's true financial condition" (Binzen and Daughen 1971: 223–224).

Other holes in the Penn Central's boundaries were probably caused or widened by irrelevant content in organizational flows. Isolated from the rest of the organization by factionalism, both alienated and buffered by his low-density relationship with Saunders and Perlman, Bevan began to develop financial activities outside the railroad. These activities paralleled his company responsibilities, and Pennphil, the investment club he cofounded, recruited a large proportion of its fifteen partners from Penn Central financial management. Not coincidentally, both Penphil and the Penn Central invested heavily in several of the same companies.

They also made loans from the same banks and hired the same consultants. One of these companies, Executive Jet Aviation, allegedly provided female "escorts" for Penn Central financial executives. In the end, the railroad lost millions of dollars on the Penphil-related investments. Ultimately, Bevan and some associates were tried and acquitted of conflict of interest charges regarding the Penphil-Penn Central connection. Whether or not their activities constituted illegal irrelevant content, there can be little doubt that the use of work contacts to build an external investment orientation influenced the boundary-maintaining function of Penn Central's finance department for the worse.

When the Penn Central's many dysfunctions finally proved fatal, death came through the usual way: The organization's boundaries collapsed, and stakeholders from the environment moved in to salvage what they could. To avoid disruption of transportation over much of the northeast, and to prevent creditors' indiscriminate pillaging of the remaining assets, Section 77 of the Bankruptcy Act permitted the road to continue operation until a new board of trustees could be appointed.

Managing Dysfunctions

In the introduction I said that I would resist the temptation to propose cures, and by and large I will keep my promise. But after presenting such a litany of woes, it would be inhumane not to offer a coping strategy or two. I will limit myself to suggestions that have some bearing on several dysfunctions at the same time.

Manage Anxiety. A lot of dysfunctional behavior in organizations comes from people's coping with their fears, real and imagined. Fearful people have excessive control and affirmation needs, and they will introduce and exploit unneeded elements in the boundaries and activity systems in an effort to satisfy those needs. They are also prone to political and ritualistic behavior. Organizations in which people feel a certain degree of trust and security avoid a host of problems. (I am indebted to Sarah Koovor Misra (1993) for this insight.)

Early Detection. You may have noticed that as we reached the end of the Penn Central case, the number and severity of dysfunctions increased dramatically. In management as in auto mechanics or medicine, one problem left to itself leads to others that lead to others. The major benefit of this chapter for managers is the ability to recognize dysfunctions early on so they don't get out of hand. Be attentive for these three warning signs that precede many dysfuctions:

1. **Decrease in directly productive activity.** High density, politicization, formalism, and other dysfunctions all deflect people's attention from doing good work. Hence, dysfunctions are usually accompanied by a decline in activities that contribute directly to attainment of organizational goals. For this reason, even minor productivity losses should get prompt attention.

2. **Increase in the proportion of informal to formal activity.** Flurries of informal activity, whether related to conflict, romance, or just horsing

around, are indicative of high density, factionalization, politicization, or ir-relevant content. Informal activity is fine if it is job related, and a certain degree of totally frivolous activity is allright, but a major increase is a bad sign.

3. Difficulty in making simple decisions. Inability of members of the organization to come to agreement about taking obviously needed mea-sures is an indication that something is slowing the organization down. Move as quickly as possible to find out where things are getting hung up in-terpersonally or procedurally and take action.

Rotate Leaders Periodically. Moving people around impedes the for-mation of factions, aids innovation and coordination, and provides a change of pace. It keeps people from hiding dirty laundry and developing little kingdoms. As long as you don't get carried away, rotation is an excel-lent vaccine for several dysfunctions.

Reward Performance, Not Noise. This is an old saw, but a good one. Few things invigorate an organization like management's accurately dis-cerning who is performing and rewarding them. Factions crumble when self interest is best served by hard work, and the drive to perform tends to point up which formal administrative mechanisms should stay and which are frivolous.

Like the common cold, crabgrass, and politicians, dysfunctions are al-most impossible to eradicate completely: but honest, vigilant management can keep them relatively minor and avoid complications. Like these com-mon plagues, however, dysfunctions do not go away if ignored. Don't let them get away from you.

3

Culture: Seeing the Invisible Boundary

Culture is a tricky thing. Evidently it is very important to organizational performance; Kotter and Heskett (1992) found that companies with strong adaptive cultures outperformed those with maladaptive cultures by hundreds of percent in both profits and stock prices. But it is also very elusive to diagnose and change. People are not trained to think in cultural terms and therefore tend to overlook ways to change the culture and may even fail to recognize its presence.

In smaller organizations, culture is especially elusive but holds special promise for those who will pay attention to it. Like the human personality and outlook on life, an organization's culture is influenced heavily by its early years and becomes progressively harder to change as it grows and ages (Kimberly and Miles 1980). This means that smaller, and particularly newer, organizations have a once-in-a-lifetime opportunity to develop the best culture possible. They are small enough to change rather quickly and easily; and if they develop a strong, healthy culture early on, its value will increase over time because larger, older competitors will be very hard-pressed to change their cultures.

Despite the comparative ease with which smaller and younger organizations can adjust, few develop ideal cultures. I believe that this happens partly because their founders don't know how to think culturally, and don't take the time necessary to suppress undesirable cultural tendencies and foment desirable ones.

Founders and CEOs are known to have an enormous impact on organizational culture (Kotter and Heskett 1992; Kets de Vries et al. 1991). Many corporations known for their strong cultures were started by strong-willed founders who stayed at the helm for many years—witness IBM, Ford, Lincoln Electric, and DuPont. Founders tend to create the organization in their own image by passing their values, attitudes, and habits (good and bad) on to subordinates. This being the case, they can cause enormous harm and good, and they usually do both.

Because founders and CEOs of small and new companies are so embroiled in day-to-day operational challenges, they have little time and energy left over to think about and explicitly deal with cultural issues. As a result, any culture that develops tends to be an uncritical extension of the values and personalities of the founders. If their particular values and personalities are consistent with the business needs of the company, much benefit will accrue. But this is rarely totally the case. Ordinarily some founder values are highly desirable and others are much less so. Moreover, the personality types that it takes to start an organization are not necessarily those that will insure its long-term health: unless organizations reassess their values periodically, they end up fighting new battles by old rules.

As an example, I know of one very hard-driving consultant who was highly time-, work-, and results-oriented, with almost no concern for personal loyalties, friendship, or painstaking analysis. In a short time he built an enormously successful consulting business offering an array of services to large corporations. He prospected vigorously for new products, tried them out for six months or so, and incorporated the successful ones into his business, discarding the rest. His approach to people was pretty much the same; he was constantly on the lookout for new associates, tried them out for awhile, and discarded the ones that didn't work as soon as difficulties arose. (The last I heard, he was on his fifth marriage.)

This "prospect, try, and scrap" mentality dominated his organization's culture, populating it with a cadre of aggressive, individualistic, fast-moving consultants. The firm grew rapidly, and it looked for a while as if it would dominate the regional industry in a number of categories. But then growth plateaued: and despite constant product innovation and feverish new business development, the company began to tread water. Turnover was astronomical, much of it due to associates who left to start competing firms. Repeat business was paltry, and most importantly, the really big contracts went to other firms.

The firm had developed a reputation as a lightweight—one that could deliver simple, standardized services quickly and efficiently, but that did not have the depth or professionalism for really important work. Particularly those divisions where creative solutions or long-term relationships were important—precisely those addressing the richest part of the market—did not do well. This company had the potential to become dominant but remained a minor player because its values never evolved from those of an aggressive upstart to those of a dominant player. Hence, the founder's values brought about a great deal of good—birthing a dynamic new force in the market—and bad, keeping his firm from maturing into a leader.

If the development of an organizational culture is not going to be haphazard—like raising a child without steady discipline, dependable emotional support, reasonable expectations, and periodic adjustments to accompany growing maturity—it must be done in a conscious, careful fashion. This chapter attempts to offer some tools that can aid such development without overloading the firm financially or psychologically.

What Is Culture?

Although you don't have to be an anthropologist to analyze and improve an organization's culture, it is important to have some idea of what is being assessed and changed. There are at least a score of different definitions of culture, and anthropologists have been debating for years which definition is best (Keesing 1974). Despite all the debate, though, most definitions agree that culture has a lot to do with how people make sense of the world around them and how they decide what things in life are worth pursuing (Gopalan 1991; O'Reily et al. 1988).

This being the case, I classify corporate culture as an organizational boundary that helps determine what ideas and values will be entertained in the organization and which will be excluded. Culture is strongest when the values of the organization are adopted by the members of the organization.

Because culture deals with ideas rather than tangibles, it is often hard to see; hence the title of this chapter, "Seing the Invisible Boundary." However, despite its ambiguity and subtlety, culture can be very important in developing shared vision, encouraging desired behaviors, and creating a reputation. In one English accounting firm that I visited, the British concept of the "gentleman" defined much of what was acceptable and desirable behavior. Hence, understatement, congeniality, good taste, confidentiality, adherence to tradition, and stable client relationships were highly valued.

This concept provided a guide for people's behavior and promoted a professional if reserved image to clients that gave great credibility to the firm. Unfortunately, it also conveyed the not-entirely-unwarranted impression that decorum and stability were preferred over responsiveness and innovation—almost the opposite of the problem that our aggressive consultant above had. As a result, as the environment of this firm changed, and it had to move from its historically stable domain to more volatile markets, it began to lose market share.

Learning to See the Invisible Boundary

The question of how culture can be accurately described and measured has been heartily debated for years, and a discussion of this debate is beyond the scope of this book (see Rousseau 1990 for an excellent review). Consistient with my overall objectives, the methods I present here are those I have found to be most compact and practical. I offer several approaches, both because the same culture can be profitably viewed from many different angles and because different cultures yield their secrets to different methods.

One key to describing a culture adequately, and therefore being able to change it, rests with two premier functions of culture: establishing categories, and deciding what is important (and by extension, what is not important). Once the British firm had clearly established the concept of "gentleman," its employees were able to classify people, ideas, and actions into the categories of gentlemanly or not-gentlemanly. It was also possible, if not unavoidable, to define gentlemanly behaviors as more important or desirable than those of the other category. With this, the world became understandable, and employees knew how to behave across a wide variety of situations.

If you know and understand the categories in your organization and can identify which categories are most desirable, you are well on your way to understanding its culture (see Cavan 1966 and Glaser and Strauss 1967 on the importance and methods of discovering categories). Another example may help clarify this discussion. Because of my mortal fear of driving anything with more than four tires, I once prevailed upon a trucker friend to drive a rented moving van full of my earthly possessions from Louisiana to Illinois. I used part of the ten hours it took driving him back home to try to figure out trucker culture. Together we identified at least ten or fifteen categories of truckers—nine-to-fivers, professionals, highway heroes, et cetera, as well as several types of truck stops and a number of categories (mostly pejorative) of nontruck drivers.

The two most enlightening categories were the high-and-low status extremes of bullhaulers and cowboys. As the name implies, bullhaulers drive trucks with cattle in them. Their attributes tell us most of what truckers consider important. The longer livestock are confined in a trailer, the more likely it is that they will sicken, die, be injured, or lose weight, so it is imperative that the bullhauler move them from point A to point B as quickly as possible. The bullhauler can be charged for damaged or expired cattle, so there is a direct link between speed and resourcefulness and financial outcomes.

Cattle can move around somewhat in the trailer, causing sudden load shifts that require very fast adjustment on the part of the driver: and cattle are full of other unpredictabilities, so agility and the ability to deal with the unexpected are important. The value of the cargo and challenges of the job mean that bullhaulers are paid well and drive newer equipment. From the foregoing we can derive those things that truckers consider most important: speed, finely tuned reflexes, ability to deal with the unexpected, responsibility for important cargo, good pay, and new equipment.

In contrast, the cowboy tells us what truckers regard as least worthy. The cowboy is an inexperienced trucker who takes needless, exhibitionist risks that are beyond his ability. Note the similarities between the two categories. Both deal with cattle and therefore are connected to the Western, macho ethic. Both deal with speed and danger, but for the bullhauler the speed and danger are inherent to the job: and someone, either an employer or a client, has recognized the driver as competent to deal with them. In the cowboy case, speed and risk are undertaken capriciously by drivers feigning abilities they do not possess. The essence of the cowboy, then, and what trucker culture disdains most, is the combination of pretense, recklessness, and self-ordained importance.

This makes sense considering the nature of the industry, especially since deregulation. The expanding demand for drivers, and the fact that almost anyone can obtain a commercial licence, lowered the entrance boundaries to the job, admitting countless upstarts not easily distinguishable from the oldtimers. Hence, greatest disapproval is reserved for those who aspire to the same status as the experienced driver without having paid their dues.

Bullhaulers and Cowboys in Organizations

How can one use categories in diagnosing organizational culture? I believe that first, you must go through the exercise of identifying what categories exist in a firm—what categories exist for customers, employees, products, work or sales strategies, and so on. Next, one should try to discover underlying properties that differentiate between categories—loyalty, speed, flexibility, aggressiveness, and so on. Then, compare the highest and lowest status categories to understand what is most valued in your organization, just as we did for the bullhaulers and cowboys. Finally, and most importantly, ask yourself if this is consistent with the domain served. Much will be entirely consistent with successful operations; cultures rarely survive over time if they are totally at variance with industry needs. However, it is normal for little vices, and sometimes even big vices, to creep into a culture, especially in firms that have been around for a while or in industries that are changing rapidly.

I have two examples of this from sales. I once did a study of the personal values and sales statistics of salesmen and women in Brazil. My data suggested that the longer a person had been working in sales, the more aggressive, time-oriented, and status-oriented they became. Ironically, these characteristics were negatively, not positively, related to sales productivity. So the longer people spent in the business, the less their values were consistent with high productivity.

Similar findings have surfaced in the United States. One anonymous company had a vision of the ideal salesperson as highly verbal and sociable, but at the same time aggressive and persistent. Over time a culture emerged that rewarded these attributes. The high-status category for this company could be described as a "pink bulldozer," the polite, friendly, and slightly exhibitionist salesperson (hence the color pink) that simply will not take "no" for an answer (hence the bulldozer).

When the company finally got around to doing empirical research on which characteristics led to sales productivity, it found that these factors were of no utility at all. In his book on sales prospecting, Bill Good (1981) makes a similar argument about the professional sales culture in the United States. He says that salespeople have been socialized to focus their energies on trying to convince people who don't want to buy to buy, rather than finding people who do; and that these values actually limit the performance of the profession.

Two More Vices and a New Approach

Establishing categories and trying to decipher their underlying properties is a useful way to gain insights about how a culture works, but it is not the only way. To illustrate a second approach to diagnosing a culture, I will use two more examples of vices. This approach rests on the idea that important categories and values often have their origins in the early history and traumas of the organization. It is more useful for older organizations with fairly distinctive histories. In this approach, rather than concentrating so much on the mental categories that can be found, we try to identify the major social groups in the organization and how they developed historically. If it is possible to identify the values of these groups, so much the better, but it is not essential. Once the groups have been identified and their history traced, we should ask again whether this state of affairs is consistent with the domain served.

The History of the Peacocks

The details of this allegory come mostly from one company, but they could easily be a composite of the experience of a number of startups of which I have some knowledge. Peacock software began not as an association of beautiful, exotic birds, but rather with the revolt of some grey and colorless pigeons fed up with slaving away writing programs for insensitive, dilettante managers who got all of the credit and most of the money.

Believing that their technical skills would be recognized by the market, they bid their employers adieu, recruited a few pigeon friends, and rented a loft in a poor section of town. For a couple a years their returns were paltry—chickenfeed, in fact. Then, almost by accident, the pigeons stumbled on an unfilled need in the market with which their particular experience and technical skills matched admirably. Through some feverish programming work and aggressive selling, they became the major supplier to a large and rich corporate market.

At this point a rather remarkable transformation overtook the pigeons. Like a butterfly emerging from the caterpillar's cocoon, they began to sprout beautiful if rather useless tailfeathers. They bought a nice building with spacious offices, established expense accounts, recruited secretaries, and leased company cars. Most importantly, they hired a flock of pigeons to write and sell software for them.

The pigeons they hired were hard-working and technically competent programmers and sellers, but they had never been involved in the kind of product development that the peacock founders had been forced to learn during their chickenfeed years. And the peacocks were tired of the pigeon business. The net result was one very successful product with a mercifully long life cycle and many upgrades, but no viable new products.

In the final analysis, the peacocks had become much like their original elitist bosses, creating a noble caste by virtue of their presence in the firm when the goose laid the golden egg, and hiring a group of subordinates to be treated as beasts of burden by virtue of their arrival after the winning product had been hatched. This two-class culture created barriers that made it impossible to come up with more winning products.

The Survivors of the Rust Bowl

In some ways this next story is just the opposite of the last one, but it is similar in its creation of a bimodal or two-class culture. Unlike Peacock software, this company never got any breaks at all. After being laid off from his job as a salesman for a sheet metal firm, Mr. Slim Pickens (not to be confused with the legendary Boone Pickens whose luck was considerably better) decided to strike out on his own.

Slim had worked his way up through the ranks at his former company and not only had a good social network from his sales years but was also a skilled and resourceful craftsman. Despite the recession that had caused his own dismissal, Slim was able to win a few bids on small government contracts and hastily went into production. He was shorthanded and ended up doing a good deal of the welding himself during the evenings. But he finished his government work on time and used the proceeds for equipment and sheet metal.

Slowly SP Manufacturing developed a reputation for good work reasonably priced, and the firm grew. But it was never easy. Slim got a good line of credit at the bank, only to have his loans called because of a financial scandal at one of his major customers. Thereafter he became very cautious about any external source of capital. He tried manufacturing a line of woodstoves for a while, but backed out when he was sued over a house fire allegedly caused by a bad stove. There were other woes: bad credit extended to a large client and cancellation of government work that had required major retooling.

All this made Slim, and his small, loyal, management cadre of many years, very cautions and somewhat fatalistic. They avoided risk, stuck to products and technologies that they knew well, and ran a financially conservative operation. Slim had two sons whom he sent to college to get engineering and business degrees, respectively. He also had a daughter who married the son of one of his longstanding customers. After short stints with other companies, both sons and the son-in-law came on board in executive positions and soon began to butt heads with the oldtimers. The heirs apparent wanted to buy new equipment, pursue new markets, take the company public, and acquire a competitor. They even wanted to change the company's name to SP International. They recruited followers among the company's younger engineers and pressed their demands constantly.

Slim and the oldtimers found the newcomers reckless, overambitous, and unappreciative of the amount of work it took to run a company. The younger faction found the oldtimers inflexible and lacking vision. Things got so bad that Slim threatened to sell the company and give his assests to charity. This cowed the heirs and their following into submission, but left them sullen and bitter.

As in the preceding example, we have reciprocal opposition in values, but instead of old peacocks and young pigeons, we have young peacocks and old pigeons. I cannot say which of the factions had the best business strategy, but it is clear that the conflict was destructive. Slim will have his way while his health holds, but he has set the company up for an ugly succession crisis when he steps down. In retrospect, it is clear that he should have worked his progeny into the company more slowly, and that his heirs should have been more patient with their desires to innovate.

The two cases discussed are typical of processes I have observed in a variety of organizations—so many, in fact, that I have begun to believe that they are almost universal. Most organizations, it seems, go through rough times, and some if not most also experience a bonanza period where things really take off. The social and cultural dynamics of firms appear to be deeply impacted by the timing of these periods and who is running the organization when they come (Bozeman and Slusher 1979; Cameron et al. 1987; Kimberly and Miles 1980). Organizations that have a fairly long boom early in their development have a tendency to develop a peacock caste of upper managers who frequently become spoiled by success and may spoil the company's long-term prospects because they never learn to fight or they retreat from the battle.

Less problematic, but also common, is the firm that has struggled against great opposition, and in the process has become so conservative and efficiency-oriented that it loses the flexibility to seize opportunities. A very common variation on this theme is the firm that becomes successful over a protracted period of struggle and whose domain actually requires a continuation of the same efficiency-oriented struggle. But with the arrival of the second generation that has not been subject to the same rigors as the first, the firm loses its edge.

In any of these cases, a careful history of the social groups in the firm will reveal the nature of the culture and the crises it faces. These cultural patterns are so common as to be quite easy for outsiders to understand and recognize. Unfortunately, however, because founders are so deep in the forest, they tend to miss these particular trees. I would recommend that any firm in existence for more than ten years have a detailed plan for detecting and handling these issues before they arise. Managers should also cultivate a friendly but frank outsider to keep the company honest. A professional consultant can fill this role, but there are cheaper alternatives such as old friends, retired competitors, newspaper reporters, and (believe it or not) government bureaucrats with knowledge of that particular industry. The key is detachment and objectivity. To fail to have concrete measures for handling these dynamics is to run the risk of trouble from dualisms, factionalism, and polarization.

A Third Approach: The Rules of the Game

Categories and social groups say a lot about the underlying fundamentals of a culture, but there is nothing like an understanding of the rules, particularly the unwritten rules of an organization, for discerning a culture. Written rules and formal regulations can provide a window on culture and should be studied if they are available. The maximum amount of money that a first-line manager can spend without approval by his or her superior speaks worlds about the culture of an organization, for instance.

Also, as important as the written rules are, much can also be learned by noting those things which are not included in the rules. For instance, the existence or nonexistence of a formal dress code is an important clue to organizational values, although not as important as actual dress practices.

One way of eliciting unwritten rules is to ask, "What is the worst possible thing you could do as a member of this organization?" This will immediately lead you to the organization's core values. Another technique is to look for regularities in behavior. Do people all arrive for meetings at the same time, or do they dribble in, from lowest to highest status? Do people leave their office doors open or closed? Do people knock before entering? Do only subordinates knock before entering? Like the uncovering of categories and the history of social groups, systematic investigation of organizational rules offers great insights into culture.

Functions and Dysfunctions of Rules

In her discussion of alcoholic families, Sharon Wegscheider (1981) discusses the functions of rules in families and sets out criteria for good rules and bad rules. I find her categories also applicable to organizations, particularly small organizations. The functions are:

1. To establish attitudes, expectations, values, and goals.
2. To determine who will hold the power and authority, how these will be used, and how members are expected to respond to them.
3. To anticipate how the family will deal with change—in itself as a unit, in its members, and in the outside world.
4. To dictate how members may communicate with one another and what they may communicate about.

This typology helps identify the functions served by the organization's rules. Rarely will you find a rule that is not somehow related to one of these categories, and a tabulation of how many organizational rules apply to each category will help reveal the relative emphasis placed on goals, authority, change, and communication in a given organization.

To decide whether a given rule is functional or dysfunctional, Wegscheider asks two questions:

1. Is the rule human or inhuman (natural or unnatural)?
2. Is the rule rigid or flexible?

Inhuman rules are those which are impossible to comply with or are damaging to the development and expression of human potential. They are dysfunctional. Similarly dysfunctional are rules that cannot account for individual differences or deal with changing conditions. I think her criteria are a useful beginning, and there is little doubt that rigid, inhuman norms are the source of much pain and misery in both families and organizations. Below I expand on her criteria somewhat, adapting them to organizational conditions I have experienced. Asking the questions posed below should provide an idea of whether a given rule is functional or dysfunctional.

Function 1. To establish attitudes, expectations, values, and goals.

Criteria for Function 1. Are attitudes, expectations, values and goals realistic? Can people reasonably be expected to comply with them? Frequently expectations and rules come about to satisfy a narcissistic image of what the world should be rather than to serve a concrete, identifiable purpose. Do rules fulfill a real need of customers or the organization, or are they purely ritualistic? Above all, are they consistent with the domain of the organization? For instance, dress codes can be totally frivolous or essential depending on whether an organization is selling Volvos or repairing them.

Function 2. To determine who will hold the power and authority, how these will be used, and how members are expected to respond to them.

Criteria for Function 2. Power and authority ideally should be related to expertise, although it is probably unrealistic to expect that power will not be influenced by proportion of ownership. In an organization with a stable domain, where the founders know the business inside out and have dealt with almost every disturbance that a fickle market can produce, it is reasonable to expect authority to be concentrated and for members to be somewhat deferential. In an organization with a broad and changing domain, power should be widely distributed and formal authority discounted (Miles and Snow 1978). Those located at the boundary of the organization should have extra clout so they can push for change as the environment requires adjustment.

Therefore it is worth asking: Are the people with the most power those with greatest knowledge and expertise? Are subordinates expected to acquiesce to superiors' orders without discussion? If so, are there good reasons for this? Do superiors see subordinates as simple extensions of the boss's will? A superior who has not actually worked in a subordinate's position needs to solicit input at least as much as he or she issues orders.

Function 3. To anticipate how the family will deal with change— in itself as a unit, in its members, and in the outside world.

Criteria for Function 3. Most organizations are highly resistant to change. There are some good reasons for this. The status quo is the product of accumulated experience, frequently over many years and much trial and error. Frequently it may also be the product of heated disagreements and conflicts that threatened to tear the organization apart, and no one may be eager to revisit those conflicts (Dahrendorf 1959). The problem, of course, is that even in the most stable environments (and there are precious few of those left), adjustments must be made to keep the firm afloat.

Although less frequent than resistance to change, the opposite does occur. Some people and organizations become fixated on change as a means of avoiding drudgery, keeping life interesting, and sometimes avoiding the discipline of regularity (Kets de Vries and Miller 1984). Aleksandr Solzhenitsyn speaks of the "cult of novelty" that drove the communists to reject all traditional values and conventions simply because they were there. Unless the organization's environment is very unstable, this can prove fatal.

For many situations I think the best balance can be obtained by declaring certain portions of the organization safe havens for experimentation. When someone has an idea for a new work process or product, send them to the backyard to try it out. Once it's working, introduce it to the troops. There are few innovations that cannot be tried out on a small scale first, but there is a tendency for people to want to see their pet projects take over the world before they have been rigorously tested. All organizations—some more than others—should have a number of funny little projects going on, and at least one in ten of them should ultimately result in a fairly large change in products or procedures. This will keep the company fresh but not crazy.

Regarding change, some pertinent questions to ask are: Is there a formal process for generating and approving new ideas? When is the last time someone in top management sponsored a change? If most change attempts come from lower down, top management is getting hidebound. Are there practices in the organization that persist despite the fact they no longer serve any useful purpose? Is there budgetary and/or physical space set apart for experimentation and innovation? What happened to the last person who proposed sweeping changes for the organization?

Function 4. To dictate how members may communicate with one another and what they may communicate about.

Criteria for Function 4. Probably the most subtle and important of functions—what is and is not open for discussion, and and how it may be approached—has profound implications for the other three functions and a host of other matters. It would be easy to argue that everything in the organization should be fair game for discussion and debate. Indeed the general trend since the liberal 1960s has been in this direction. The feeling has been that disclosure is healthy, and restraint is unhealthy because it "bottles things up" that will eventually get out in one way or another. Moreover, if problems are disclosed immediately they are easier to handle, while they tend to explode or return in perverse new incarnations if left to fester.

The sentiment for disclosure speaks to the perennial problem of denial in human existence (Pauchant and Mitroff 1992). The fact that we make mistakes, die, or have various limitations is unpleasant, so we tend to try to hide the facts from ourselves and others where possible (Janis 1982). The bigger the problem, the stronger the propensity toward denial, so people and organizations with more problems tend to deny more. The denial process sucks up large amounts of mental and physical resources, leaving us less energy to deal with problems and thereby exacerbating our difficulties further. Additional difficulties call for further denial, and so on. Logically, then, the less our rules restrict the subject matter and delivery of communication, the less denial and better health our organization will have.

The problem with this "let it all hang out" approach is the equally valid and somewhat more longstanding tradition of decorum, courtesy, tact, and self-control which have been the hallmark of civilized societies for millennia. One of the things that enable us to survive in communities is a certain restraint in expressing observations, impulses, wishes, and instinctual inclinations. Some Freudians go so far as to argue that the repression and denial of fundamental primitive urges create the essential pressure that moves the higher manifestations of civilized life. There is also the matter, more crucial to businesses, that thinking about all the things that can go wrong or all the things that are wrong with the business can create a self-fulfilling prophecy of doom that ensures defeat.

Without proposing to resolve the dialectics of human society for the past two thousand years, let me offer some suggestions for balancing restraint and candor. First, there are reasons why all varieties of intimacy have been closely regulated in human societies that have survived for long periods, and it is unlikely that your organization is going to be the first one to successfully dispense with those regulations.

Second, communicate about both strengths and weaknesses of competitors. A very common form of denial in many companies is a norm that requires employees only to speak of competitors in pejorative terms (Janis 1982). It is important for firms to make gossip about competitors' moves a pastime. At least a portion of the space that every firm dedicates to tinkering and innovation should be allocated to copying competitors' strengths or capitalizing on their weaknesses.

Third, communicate about money and performance. For many firms, information about the financial condition of the firm and the disposition of its funds is closely held by a few managers. Information that is not confidential—and a certain amount of it will be—should be widely disseminated and discussed. This information, whether negative or positive, focuses thought and effort, provides a sense of ownership, motivates savings, and spurs performance.

Fourth, don't punish the bearer of bad news. Make it clear that each employee has both the right and the obligation to call attention to problems and dilemmas. Admission of mistakes should be expected from everyone, irrespective of their place in the hierarchy. Fifth, don't cry over spilled milk. Once a decision has been made and a course taken, discussion and debate should cease and action begin.

The following questions provide for introspection about communication processes: Is information treated as a scarce good or does it flow freely? Do communication practices and norms support a sense of professionalism, mutual respect, and decorum? Do your norms exclude from discussion personal concerns unrelated to the performance of the organization? If they don't, you may be a prime candidate for irrelevant content in your flows (see Chapter 2). Do people feel reasonably comfortable about communicating negative information to superiors? Is honesty in the admission of mistakes interpreted as a sign of strength and professionalism? Do norms encourage ample and honest communication with clients?

4

CVAT: A Fourth Approach

The approaches covered in Chapter 3 are well suited for those adept at searching for invisible categories, unwritten rules, and interpretive history, and every company should do some soulsearching of this type at least once. Moreover, an understanding of the mental and social categories of a firm is necessary in planning to change an organization's culture. But there is something undeniably fuzzy about the approaches discussed, and they will not come naturally to managers who do not have a lot of time and inclination for reflection.

The approach I offer now is a good deal quicker and less ambiguous, but it lacks the richness of the more narrative approaches. On the other hand, it generates a wealth of precise, easily understood statistics that can be applied to a number of different cultural and interpersonal situations. I have used the approach myself for a number of years and have sold it to many larger organizations.

The Culture and Value Analysis Tool (CVAT for short) is an approach to culture that combines the social groups perspective of our second approach with the third fact of organizational life stated in Chapter 1 (there are trade-offs). The social groups aspect of the CVAT is somewhat secondary, so I will dedicate most of my efforts to how culture can be discerned by analyzing how organizations and people handle trade-offs. Later on I will discuss how CVAT uncovers the social groups in an organization by locating regularities in people's perceptions of culture. Portions of this explanation are taken from the CVAT instruction manual, which contains a more detailed treatment of this particular approach.

Trade-Offs and Culture

It is well known that people cannot entertain more than one thought at a time (Organ and Bateman 1992). Our memory and recall abilities are also limited. Given the finite amount of time and mental processing capacity humans have, this means that we are limited in the variety and number of concepts we can deal with. As a result we end up selecting, from the infinite array of stimuli that bombard us constantly, a relatively small number of interests and concerns to attend to. Culture helps define what things will hold our attention and interest. By process of elimination, culture also determines what we will not attend to. In short, culture tells us what things are worth worrying about and what things aren't.

If I am correct in my belief that a major function of culture is to select which of life's many conflicting possibilities will get priority (and much anthropological thought agrees with this view), then describing a culture is fairly simple, if not easy. We need only identify those things that cultural systems have to choose between, and ask people in the organization to tell us what the organization's choices are. Identifying the choices that all cultural systems have to make is both difficult and easy. It is difficult because the great variability in cultures assures that no matter hard one tries, any instrument is going to leave something out. Sense of style is important at beauty salons, devotion is important at churches, precision is important for accounting firms. But any of these dimensions is probably too narrow for a generic measure of culture.

On the other hand, if one looks for very broad choices, it is quite easy to find universal themes that virtually every organization contains. In searching for functions common to all human systems, I repeatedly came across three: work (also called "task"), relations, and control, frequently associated with power or politics. Moreover, these three functions are at odds in much of the scholarly literature and popular folklore. The tension between task and relationships is found in the myth and literature of all cultures and was constantly contrasted in the midcentury management literature of the United States (see, for instance, Blake and Mouton 1964; Larson et al. 1976; Nystrom, 1978).

Power or control is at least as ubiquitous as Work and Relations, and is usually seen in opposition to one of the two. David McClelland (1961) identifies a need for achievement, need for affiliation, and need for power as the basic forces underlying human motivation. These concepts are almost identical to the concepts of task, relations, and control. McClelland too tends to see the three forces as antagonistic. Alderfer (1969) also identifies three basic needs (existence, relatedness, and growth) which can be loosely related to power or security, relations, and task achievement.

In addition to these three very fundamental themes, I have included a fourth category, that is, cognition or thought. Particularly in business organizations, it seemed to me that reflection and rationality are important themes that often clash with other values. While thought may not be one of the fundamental needs, it is important. As Freud said, "The voice of the intellect is soft but persistent."

Subdimensions

Once general cultural themes are identified, a number of subthemes suggest themselves. These are usually contradictory but occasionally complementary. In order to keep the questionnaire balanced, I chose four subdimensions for each major dimension, resulting in sixteen themes in all. For work, the subdimensions are effort, time orientation, finishing tasks, and quality. Effort deals with emphasis on hard work. Time orientation deals with regard for deadlines, schedules, and speed. Finishing tasks deals with emphasis on bringing projects to a conclusion; and quality, of course, deals with the quality of outputs. Time pressures and the need for task completion tend to lower quality, whereas effort supports all three subdimensions.

The relations quadrant consists of affect, empathy, sociability, and loyalty. These subdimensions relate to voluntary connections with other people, but each has a different emphasis. Affect brings one close to others, principally to take nurturance. Empathy brings closeness—but to give nurturance. Sociability focuses on closeness and interaction with groups of people rather than individuals. Loyalty emphasizes durable, long-lasting relations of mutual obligation to people or groups. These subdimensions are not inherently contradictory, but neither are they necessarily mutually reinforcing. People with strong affective needs are not necessarily empathetic, loyal, or sociable. Sociability does not presume empathy or loyalty (one can move from one party to another and still be quite sociable). Loyalty does not presume empathy, although it does not preclude it.

The four subdimensions of control represent different influence strategies. Dominance involves imposing one's will openly without contrivance. Status favors one's will, or at least one's ego, by creating or highlighting symbolic inequalities between individuals. Politics or manipulation involves getting one's way through manipulation and contrivance, while Leadership secures control through charisma or "referent power" (French and Raven 1962). Although all four approaches are present in all societies and cultures, Leadership appears to be the only one universally tolerated if not revered.

Under Cognition or Thought we have Abstraction, Planning/Organization, Exposition, and Flexibility. While Abstraction deals with generalities, Planning and Organization tends to focus on details. Exposition is another domain entirely, dealing not with the production of ideas but rather with their transmission. Flexibility is another rather unrelated item, but one which consistently comes up in discussions of individual creativity, organizational adaptability, and national survival. Once dimensions of some kind have been identified, the only real hurdle is finding a practical way to get people to communicate how their organizations prioritize them. One very quick way of doing this is by using the Culture Matrix found in Figure 4.1. We create a matrix or box in which the rows list the subdimensions from the Work and Relations quadrants, and the Columns list the subdimensions from the Control and Thought quadrants. By definition, each cell or space in the matrix will confront or intersect two subdimensions. For instance, the upper left hand cell (row 1 and column 1) sets Effort off against Dominance.

Figure 4.1 Culture Matrix Responses for Politicized University

	Have Your Way	Status	Political (Wheeler-Dealer)	Leadership	Theory/ Analysis	Organization/ Details	Exposition/ Presentation	Flexibility/ Risk Taking	Total
Hard Work	←	←	←	←	←	←	←	←	0
Time	←	←	←	←	←	←	←	←	0
Finish Job	←	←	←	←	←	←	←	←	0
Quality	←	←	←	←	←	←	←	←	0
Warmth	←	←	←	←	←	←	←	←	0
Empathy	←	←	←	←	←	←	←	←	0
Sociability	↑	←	←	↑	↑	↑	↑	↑	6
Loyalty	↑	←	←	↑	←	↑	←	↑	4
	6	8	8	6	7	6	7	6	

The lower right hand cell (row 8, column 8) juxtaposes Loyalty with Flexibility. We ask our respondent to start with the first row, and ask himself whether the row property or the column property is seen as most important in the organization. If the row property takes precedence, a horizontal arrow should be placed in the appropriate space. If a column property takes precedence, a vertical arrow should be used.

So, if Effort is more highly regarded than Dominance (obedience) in my organization, I would put a horizontal arrow in the upper left hand space. If Status is more important than Effort, I would put a vertical arrow in the second space in the first row and so on. Once the entire matrix has been filled out, our respondent will have compared the importance of each dimension with eight of the other dimensions. This will provide a fair idea of what our respondent thinks is most valued in the organization. In Figure 4.1, I have filled out the culture matrix for a university I know well.

These responses are easily summarized and presented in graph form (see Figure 4.2), We simply sum the number of horizontal arrows at the end of each row and sum the number of vertical arrows at the bottom of each column. For instance, in Figure 4.1 we see that effort received zero out of eight possible points, indicating minimal emphasis on rewards for hard work. In column three, dealing with politics, the sum was eight, indicating a highly politicized environment. The comparative importance of each dimension is seen when we plot the score for each dimension on the same axis as seen in Figure 4.2. Blank copies of both the matrix and the profile form are provided in Appendix 2 of this book.

We can see from the graph that this organization is highly oriented toward the control and thought quadrants, with almost no concern for work, and mixed concern for relations. The combination of high politics and status, with moderate loyalty and sociability, and little concern for quality and effort, indicates a paternalistic, inward-looking organization with much more concern for distribution of resources and honors that for the wellbeing of its employees or service to its domain. A profile like this suggests the likely presence of several dysfunctions, most likely politicization and irrelevant content. The emphasis on status and control also suggests frivolous complexity to provide honorific titles and regulate conflict.

Weaknesses of the Culture Matrix Approach

The method I have described has a couple of drawbacks that require a somewhat more sophisticated format to cure. First, it will be difficult for many respondents to imagine exactly what is meant by, say, dominance, or sociability, or flexibility. It is also likely that what one respondent understands by abstraction may be different from what another understands. The best way to handle this is to provide phrases for people to rate rather than

Figure 4.2   Culture Matrix for Politicized University

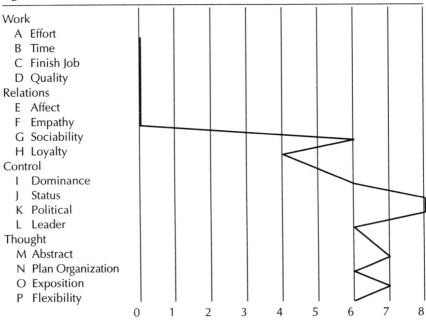

just dimensions. So, instead of simply guessing whether sociability or dominance are most favored, we ask the respondent to choose between the statements "In this organization it is important to be a good host" and "Obedience to rules is important here." If we do this a number of times with somewhat similar phrases, our responses will be much more accurate.

The other problem is that the culture matrix method described above contrasts each dimension with only half of the other dimensions. Thus, there is no guarantee that the profile would be the same if a complete contrast were undertaken. To do this with the version in your copy of this book would require a complex and rather ungainly matrix format that makes completing and scoring the instrument somewhat confusing. Despite its drawbacks, the method does provide some systematic information, and the Appendix provides instructions for calculating summary statistics for the culture matrix using a shareware program available from the author. It takes a little work, but its probably the cheapest way available to get a profile of an organization's culture.

I have developed another format for generating a statistical profile of the organization's culture that overcomes the two drawbacks described above. It is called CVAT, for Culture and Value Analysis Tool: it comes with a very powerful, user-friendly software package that allows data entry, performs calculations, provides statistics, and plots profiles, and does other important things with very little effort on the part of the operator. The CVAT questionnaires have been used extensively in research on organizational culture and have been subjected to a number of tests to ascertain their validity. If you plan to embark on a serious culture diagnosis, you would be better off using the CVAT, which can be bought for about a fourth of the average consultant's daily fee. Other similar instruments are available, albeit for higher prices. The examples and statistics cited from this point on use CVAT data, but they can be interpreted exactly as you would interpret the culture matrix data.

Uses of the Culture Matrix/CVAT Aprroach

Once you understand the basic principle behind the Culture Matrix/CVAT, a number of possibilities open up, because the same principles and procedures that are used to describe the present state of a firm's culture can be applied to other pertinent concerns. The same technique can be used to describe the way people would like a culture to be. A slight variation on the method also generates profiles of personal values that can then be contrasted to the real and ideal culture profiles. And there is nothing to keep you from having subordinates or peers describe what they perceive to be each others' personal values.

Taken together, these different types of information can yield a wealth of useful data about the organization and the people in it. In addition to the analysis of goals, boundaries, and activity systems, the culture considered ideal by members of the organization can be an important guide to how the culture should be oriented. The location of differences in what employees would have as a preferred culture is indicative of the presence of important social groups and possibly even subcultures. Working through these differences can be an important part of developing a healthy culture.

The difference between an employee's ideal culture and the real or perceived culture can also be an important indicator of where the culture needs to change and what organizational values are ready to be changed. Similarly, locating groups whose ideal culture is most distant from what they see as the real culture can be an important clue to where problems will develop in the organization.

Because individuals in a small organization can have a strong influence on its culture, it is important to know the values of the major players in the firm and how they relate to the desired culture. This can help founders and others to be introspective about the impact of their personal style on the organization's culture. It can also be useful to look at the personal values of the firm as a whole, as it is common for companies to hire a certain type of individual without really thinking about the opportunities and the limitations this places on the development of a corporate culture.

Conflict between individuals can cause a disproportionate amount of damage in a small organization, and these conflicts often originate in personal value differences. Therefore, an understanding of individual values, particularly on the part of partners and others whose relationship with each other can influence firm performance, can be very useful. Additionally, the development of corporate culture is frequently influenced by the conflicts and antagonisms that take place between major players and their values, providing another reason why it can be useful to have an understanding of personal values.

Examples

I will now provide examples of these uses and how they can interlock. I will begin with the last category of data, the individual level, because people are the building blocks of any culture and because no example of personal value data has yet been given. Moreover, understanding co-workers and subordinates is probably one of the most important things that any manager can do.

Collecting data on individuals uses the same form as organization culture except that we ask what values take precedence for the individual rather than what values take precedence in the organization. My personal responses appear in Table 4.1.

My profile shows a workaholic (a score of 8 out of 8 for hard work) concerned about doing things on time and getting projects finished (7 of 8 possible on the time and finish job dimensions). Quality is important (6 of 8) but not as important as finishing things on time. Unlike my work life (quadrant 1), which is internally consistent and takes precedence over all other spheres of existence, my emotional or relations quadrant is mixed. It is obvious that I am an absolute hermit (sociability) when it comes to doing things with groups or collectives. On the other hand, loyalty is clearly important to me as well as empathy, and, to a lesser degree, affect.

It is not unusual for people to rate differently on different items of the same quadrant. It permits them to hold stock in all areas of life without becoming overcommitted to any one quadrant. Looking at the differences within a quadrant provides an idea of the person's particular way of coping with that aspect of life. The profile suggests that I retreat from group life but compensate by having very strong loyalties to individuals and trying to be helpful when I can (empathy = 6). In the thought quadrant, I am quite analytical (theory, 6 out of 8) but uniformly lukewarm in other areas, suggesting that I do a lot of thinking but not much organizing or conveying my thoughts to others.

Table 4.1   Culture Matrix—Personal Profile of Reed Nelson

Self	
8	Effort
7	Time
7	Finish Job
6	Quality
4	Affect
6	Empathy
1	Sociability
8	Loyalty
1	Dominance
2	Status
0	Politics
1	Leadership
6	Abstraction
3	Detail/Organization
2	Exposition
3	Flexibility

When any one quadrant is consistently high or low, there is a danger of imbalance. This is clearly the case in my work and control quadrants. My control quadrant is extremely weak across the board, which means I often get used as a doormat and feel betrayed because of my high loyalty needs. I also feel that I work hard but don't get a full share of the rewards of my labors because of insufficient assertiveness.

The fact that a person is unbalanced, as I am, does not mean he cannot be successful or that he should change. Often a person or even an organization that emphasizes one quadrant or subdimension very strongly can leverage this over emphasis into a personal or corporate competitive advantage. But there is little doubt that a cost will have to be paid in terms of difficulty in dealing with quadrants that are deemphasized.

It is important to look at any person or culture in terms of its total configuration of values, not just relationships between dimensions within or between quadrants (O'Reily et al. 1988). This can be done by asking the possible meaning of the highest scores compared to the lowest scores—the peaks and valleys. Doing this for my case suggests (in addition to the insights already posed) that my work and loyalty ethic would make me a hardworking, dependable, if somewhat gullible, employee who would excel in individual or one-on-one situations that require empathy and reflection, but would fail in highly visible or political pursuits.

My individual profile using the culture matrix technique is compared to my CVAT individual value profile in Table 4.2.

The overall dimensions are similar, except that the shorter culture matrix approach seems to generate more extreme values. (Note that the CVAT graphic is round, making it easier to sense the dynamic interplay between variables.) Given that the culture matrix is of more recent vintage and less exhaustive than the CVAT techniques, it should probably be taken less seriously. A good policy in either case is to focus on the high and low values, assuming that middle-range values suggest that the particular dimension in question is not central to the values of a given individual or culture.

By themselves, these individual profiles are useful for personal reflection and possibly job placement and career planning, but there are much better, more thoroughly developed personal assessment instruments on the market. However, by combining the individual instruments with their organizational counterparts, a more synergistic view of both the organization and its members can be had. I now demonstrate a number of ways these instruments can be used to shed light on co-worker relations and organizational values.

Comparing Individual Profiles

Comparing co-worker profiles side by side can be a real revelation, as can filling out a profile for each others' values. (This should be done only if you have a fairly trusting relationship and are comfortable discussing personality issues. If you're already at each others' throats, avoid this. Instead, seek out a neutral professional for counseling.) Table 4.3 displays the profile of my wife of fifteen years plotted against mine.

A quick glance above sheds light on the major sticking points in our relationship. She enjoys groups and social events, while I want to stay home and discuss philosophy with a maximum of one or two friends (compare sociability and theory dimensions). I go into apoplexy if we are five minutes late, while punctuality is a secondary concern for her (see the time dimension).

Of course, not all of the sticking points are because of our differences. Neither of us is very dominant, so we fight about who is going to call the landlady about the leaky roof. Similarly, neither of us is very organized, so the bank statement rarely gets balanced. In marriage, as in a business, one needs to have strengths that complement the other's weaknesses but also enough areas of agreement to be able to form common ground.

Comparing Our Perceptions with Others'

The deeper conversations come from a comparison of our self-perception with others' perceptions of us. Table 4.4 is a repeat of the personal value pro-

Table 4.2   Culture Matrix Versus CVAT—Personal Profile of Reed Nelson

20	8	Effort
18	7	Time
14	7	Finish Job
18	6	Quality
14	4	Affect
10	6	Empathy
6	1	Sociability
12	8	Loyalty
11	1	Dominance
10	2	Status
5	0	Politics
9	1	Leadership
18	6	Abstraction
9	3	Detail/Organization
15	2	Exposition
11	3	Flexibility

Table 4.3   Culture Matrix Personal Profile of Rosemary and Reed Nelson

Rose	Reed	
7	8	Effort
3	7	Time
8	7	Finish Job
8	6	Quality
8	4	Affect
8	6	Empathy
5	1	Sociability
8	8	Loyalty
0	1	Dominance
0	2	Status
0	0	Politics
1	1	Leadership
1	6	Abstraction
2	3	Detail/Organization
2	2	Exposition
2	3	Flexibility

Table 4.4   Culture Matrix Personal Profile of Reed Nelson by Self and by Wife

Wife	Self	
6	8	Effort
6	7	Time
8	7	Finish Job
6	6	Quality
3	4	Affect
3	6	Empathy
2	1	Sociability
8	8	Loyalty
1	1	Dominance
3	2	Status
0	0	Politics
6	1	Leadership
6	6	Abstraction
3	3	Detail/Organization
3	2	Exposition
0	3	Flexibility

file done by me next to my wife's version of my personal profile. (She filled out a profile of my values without any knowledge of my own responses.)

Rose sees me as a little less interested in working hard and a little more interested in getting things done than I do. She also sees me as much more leader-oriented and less flexible and empathetic. When we discussed these differences in perceptions, I realized that I filled out the matrix thinking mostly of my professional experience rather than our home life. This makes me realize how generally my professional concerns take precedence over domestic needs (something she claimed to be aware of already). It also occurred to me that some of my home behaviors could be exported profitably to the work setting, and vice versa. The disparity in self/other perception also led to a discussion of each other's concept of empathy. It turned out that because of our different cultural backgrounds, our definitions of empathy and how it is expressed were somewhat different.

Conversations like this can be very useful in understanding daily incidents in a relationship, communicating clearly, and negotiating acceptable compromises about fundamental disagreements. Again I must stress, though, that this kind of soulsearching is more for preventive maintenance than for crisis intervention. Discussions of values and styles need to be undertaken fairly early in a relationship, after some mutual understanding and trust have been gained but before goodwill and patience have been seriously strained by conflicts or by the daily crush of doing business.

The Individual-Culture Interface

Ultimately, what we value as individuals will influence what we want our organizations to value. This fact has a host of implications for the development of organizational culture and for people's relations to that culture, not to mention their own morale and psychological adjustment. These dynamics are well illustrated in the profiles of a CEO and VP for human resources of a large manufacturing concern.

For years, this family-held company had been the market leader for a common consumer durable. The company had a strong paternalistic flavor and many cliques. The president, whose profiles we will examine, is the first nonfamily member to run the firm. He saw his basic mission as that of professionalizing the firm and bringing it into the twentieth century. At the time the profiles were taken, the firm was competing head to head with an aggressive upstart company that had flooded the market with a stripped down yet functional model that was much cheaper than those offered by other manufacturers. The VP for human resources had been hired away from a young company with a reputation for very progressive, almost utopian, personnel practices. Table 4.5 shows the personal value profiles of each executive compared with their desired or ideal organizational culture.

The most striking difference between the two personal profiles is found in the relations quadrant, where the personnel director exhibits uniformly high values compared to the president's more mixed profile. (Recall our earlier discussion of the potential difficulties associated with very high values consigned to one quadrant.) Particularly empathy, sociability, and loyalty are much higher for the VP for human resources than for the CEO, who is particularly low in the affect and sociability area. Other significant differences are found in the cognition quadrant, where the CEO is particularly high in planning/organization and exposition. The CEO is also more effort-oriented and more dominant. Given the considerable disparities in personal values between the two executives, one would expect to find considerable disparities in personal viewpoints and perceptions.

Moving to profiles of the ideal culture, we can see that while these are not a simple extension of personal values, there is a clear relationship between the two profiles. In the last column of Table 4.5 I have indicated those dimensions for which both the individual values and ideal culture of one person are higher than those of the other with an "I." "I" stands for isomorphism, meaning that the personal and ideal organizational values match or fit each other. Particularly in the relationship quadrant, personal and ideal values follow each other closely. In the control quadrant, both parties are in substantial agreement despite their differences in personal values. Both agree that leadership rather than dominance, status, or politics should be the major control strategy for the firm.

Table 4.5   Personal Values and Ideal Cultures of Two Executives

Personal Values		Ideal Culture		
CEO	VP/HR	CEO	VP/HR	
16	11	12	9 I	Effort
6	8	12	9	Time
9	10	17	15	Finish Job
15	15	18	16	Quality
8	12	11	15 I	Affect
12	18	15	18 I	Empathy
8	16	12	14 I	Sociability
14	18	11	19 I	Loyalty
16	12	5	5	Dominance
6	9	6	6	Status
12	6	9	8 I	Politics
19	17	17	14 I	Leadership
14	13	15	13 I	Abstraction
18	10	17	10 I	Detail/Organization
16	11	12	12	Exposition
11	13	11	17 I	Flexibility

Looking at all of the values at once we can compose a narrative that adds some richness to the profile and lets the numbers talk to us. The CEO is a hard-working, highly organized, verbal type who likes to lead, likes to have his way and is willing to do some politicking to get it. (See the effort, planning/organization, exposition, leadership, dominance, and politics dimensions.) He is not terribly time-oriented, nor does he care much for status or group activities. He wants to see an organization with strong leaders, decisive decisionmaking, strong planning, and strong organization. Analysis and empathy would also be favored.

The human resource VP is highly loyal, empathetic, and group-oriented. She also relishes leadership roles, but is not as effort- or planning-oriented as the CEO and she abhors politics. In her ideal organization, loyalty and empathy would predominate, while planning, work, and time would take a back seat. Leadership would not take a predominant role, but flexibility would be valued, and decisiveness cultivated, though to a lesser degree. A possible summary statement of the VP-HR's ideal organization would be, "If we take care of relationships, everything else will take care of itself." Stated in these terms, it is a far cry from the more aggressive, mechanistic view of the CEO.

This story has a rather sad ending. Under the pressures of competition from the low-priced newcomer, the president undertook a thorough reorganization and downsizing of the firm. The VP of human resources and a number of other executives were replaced in the purge. When I compared the profiles of the dismissed executives with those who were retained, I found that the retained employees had an ideal profile much closer to the president's than those dismissed. Interestingly, there was not a major difference between the personal values of the retained and dismissed persons.

Individual-Culture Issues

This case points up some interesting aspects of the individual-culture interface and raises a number of issues. As I affirmed at the beginning of this section, it demonstrates how personal values influence organizational culture and how differences in personal values can overlap into the cultural arena. It seems that, particularly in those personal-value dimensions held very strongly, the ideal culture tends to be similar. I have statistically verified the isomorphic relationship pointed out for the CEO, VP, and for the rest of the employees in the firm studied as well as a number of other cases. Indeed, more often than not, disagreements about an organization's optimal culture are founded on differences in personal values. Not surprisingly, this case, as well as other research (O'Reily et al. 1988), suggests that when individual values clash with corporate values, stress and turnover are likely.

At the same time that this case demonstrates isomorphism between individual values and desired culture, it demonstrates that what people value personally is not always what they want their organization to value. For instance, both the CEO and the VP-HR are fairly dominant but do not relish dominance in the organization. Conversely, the VP-HR does not value flexibility personally as much as she does organizationally. To me, this disjuncture between personal and organizational values highlights the need for top managers to consciously examine how their personal styles may be getting in the way of the organizational culture they want to develop. If they do not have a clear idea of their personal values and of the values they want to see in their organization (such as that provided by the CVAT), they are unlikely to see where gaps exist between the two and to take measures to assure that their personality does not have a negative impact on the organization.

Harmony Versus Heterogeneity

One of the thorny issues that surfaces here as well as elsewhere in this book, is the trade-off between culture strength, harmony, and homogeneity. The departure of those endorsing a different ideal culture favors consensus about ideal culture and ultimately a stronger culture. It also means less conflict about cultural and other questions. The downside is a loss of diversity of perspectives in the organization and possible rejection of novel ideas. The tension between these factors is reflective of the basic tensions between efficiency, flexibility, and harmony mentioned in Chapter 2, and it is found in a variety of contexts, one of the most noticeable being that of comparative national cultures.

Japan is noted for a highly homogeneous and harmonious society where individuals are taught to make great sacrifices for the common good and for the honor of the extended clan. In CVAT terms, we have a society where loyalty and effort are valued. This has facilitated the production of very high quality merchandise for very reasonable prices (Ouchi 1981). At the same time it leads to great homogeneity, which has put an extraordinary damper on creativity, such that Japan has been very low in Nobel prizes and new product development when compared to its technical and capital prowess. By contrast, the United States and France, with highly individualistic cultures, have the opposite problem: they have been sources of great creativity but are hindered by lack of consensus and community and by frequent litigation and conflict.

The comparative advantages and dangers in choosing the trade-off between homogeneity and flexibility are influenced by several factors. Two common but seldom noted considerations are the tenure of the dominant coalition (academese for the top management cadre) and the degree of stress faced by the organization. When a firm first opens for business or a new management group takes over, there is a natural period of goodwill during which cooperation is forthcoming, positions are flexible, and consensus is easily reached. Over time, positions harden, conflict surfaces, and consensus becomes more difficult to maintain.

Purges and Stress

The aging process in any social group usually means eventual turnover, and those who leave have a different ideal vision of the group than the main power holders. This turnover process usually begins with those who differ most radically and cannot reconcile their vision with that of the majority (Greenhalgh 1982; Janis 1982; Weitzel and Johnson 1989). The result of these initial departures is greater consensus and higher morale among those staying. Because those who depart probably hold positions that are so distant from those of the majority that acceptance is impossible, initial departures are probably good for getting the organization off dead center.

As time goes on, the social unit continues to age, and other conflicts arise, there is a tendency for the leadership to resort to yet more purges to solidify its position and facilitate consensus. (The process is probably observed most easily in the periodic reshuffling of cabinets in national governments.) However, successive purges tend to distance or silence those whose positions are not highly deviant, thereby depriving the organization of important creative and innovative tendencies. Put differently, the first purges get rid of the kooks, but successive purges eliminate normal people with a mind of their own that keep the organization from stagnation.

The ideal balance between flexibility and harmony will depend on the breadth and volatility of the organization's domain. But the tendency for successive purges as management cadres age suggests that to avoid damaging the firm's adaptive capabilities, departures of key players should be fewer as time goes on. If changes do have to be made, replacements should be sought whose values and opinions are at least as divergent from the majority as the party departing.

The natural tendency for organizations to become too homogeneous in response to the natural tendency toward discord can be greatly exacerbated by stressors like financial duress, downsizing, or loss of market share. Scholars have noticed a tendency for systems to become more rigid, centralized, and authoritarian when they are threatened (Straw et al. 1981). Dissent is squelched, and loyalty becomes paramount. So efficacious is an external crisis in consolidating power that wars have been fought less for territorial or foreign policy ends than to prop up a tottering regime (the Falkland Islands conflict is one of many possible examples).

If a crisis leads to staff reduction, the pressure to dismiss dissidents can be very great indeed. For this reason, the older and more stressed an organization or management team, the more vigilance must be exercised to avoid excessive homogeneity and foster independent thinking.

The principles discussed up to this point can be summarized by posing a few primary rules of organizational culture:

1. Who you are influences how you influence culture.
2. If you do not plan how you will influence your culture, you will end up influencing it in ways you did not intend.
3. When personal and organizational values do not match, stress and turnover occur.
4. As social units age they tend to become dysfunctionally homogeneous.
5. When exposed to stress, social units tend to become dysfunctionally rigid and homogeneous.
6. When old social units are exposed to stress, they are highly likely to respond dysfunctionally.

Culture Strength, Culture Content, and Organizational Effectiveness

The principles entertained above lead logically to a discussion of the strength and content of organizational cultures. A culture's strength can be defined as its ability to influence people's thinking and behavior. When we talk about the specific ways a culture influences thinking and behavior, we are talking about its content. Two organizations can have very strong cultures with very different content. For instance, both the Mafia and the FBI are noted for great uniformity in behavior and beliefs, but the content of those behaviors and beliefs are quite different.

Conversely, organizations can have weak cultures with similar content, as might be the case with two competing car dealerships with high turnover. It is important for managers to have an idea of their culture's strength, because one of the surest ways of influencing a culture is by strengthening or weakening it.

In organizations with strong cultures, we find considerable uniformity in thought and behavior without the need for formal control mechanisms and close supervision to assure compliance. Such uniformity can be a tremendous asset in service businesses or other contexts where it is difficult but important to monitor the nuances of employee behavior.

This does not mean, however, that stronger cultures are always superior. When organizational culture first became a fad in the late 1970s it was believed that strong cultures automatically led to strong performance. This view has since been discredited as researchers found a number of organizations with strong but dysfunctional cultures. In retrospect it seems clear that it is not enough for people to think and behave similarly; they have to think and behave in a way that is useful to the firm. And, in view of our observations on homogeneity and flexibility, it would also seem that a culture can become so strong that it prejudices organizational adaptation.

All this raises four important questions:

1. How do we know what culture content is best for our organization?
2. How do we know what culture strength is best for our organization?
3. How can we tell whether our organization's culture is healthy?
4. How can we tell whether our culture's strength is appropriate?

As usual, I will try to address these questions using cases. These cases will again rely heavily on CVAT data to describe culture. In addition to my natural proclivity to use a method that I know and trust, there is a reason for this. The first two approaches to culture we discussed in the last chapter deal only with culture content. That is, they only describe what categories or social groups exist, not the intensity with which they are experienced. There are indeed some qualitative (i.e., non-numerical) ways of measuring culture strength, but they are so specialized and cumbersome that they do not merit discussion in a book of this scope. CVAT and other statistically-based culture diagnostics measure both strength and content and can be manipulated to identify social groups. Because we are interested in both content and strength and how they interrelate, we need to take an approach that looks at both simultaneously.

Introducing the "Real" Profile

The case below introduces a third type of CVAT data, the "real" or "descriptive" profile of the organization's values. The appliance manufacturer case dealt only with personal values and the ideal cultural profile. The real profile uses the same dimensions as the other two, and in fact uses the same phrases as the ideal profile, but the respondent is instructed to describe the organization as he or she currently perceives it rather than as he or she would like it to be. The real profile is vital for gauging where the organization's culture is now and locating pockets of comparative satisfaction and dissatisfaction. Together with the ideal profile, it indicates which aspects of the culture the employees feel need most work.

Two Restaurants

The CVAT data below are from two restaurants, both belonging to the same owner, both with similar locations, clientele, identical menu offerings, and equal numbers of employees. One of the two, however, has a durable reputation for better food and service. It also has considerably less turnover than the other. Looking at Table 4.6, can you guess which is which?

The answer is of course unit A. A number of very obvious hints point in that direction. But there also are also aspects of the data that the untrained eye would miss and that have implications for our four questions above. I will start with the more obvious items and progress to the more subtle differences.

The descriptive profile shows that unit A emphasizes effort, finishing tasks, and quality more than unit B. We would expect these characteristics to favor better overall performance if not reduced turnover. The highest mean for unit B is politics, for A it is dominance. The other dimensions of the control quadrant are about the same for both restaurants. This result suggests that both units are highly control-oriented, but that in unit A control is explicit, while in B it is the object of subterfuge and manipulation (i.e., the political dimension). If there is one cultural dimension that is universally associated with conflict and poor performance, it is politics (remember our discussion of politicization as a dysfunction in Chapter 2). In all cases I have studied, people prefer naked dominance to politics.

There are two other large differences between A and B. B is higher than A in both sociability and exposition. Why these components of culture content would be associated with lower performance and turnover may not be immediately apparent until one considers their likely relationship to politics. In

Table 4.6   Organization Culture in Two Restaurants

Real		Ideal		
A	B	A	B	
14.0	12.2	14.6	14.0	Effort
13.7	13.8	11.9	11.6	Time
13.8	12.5	12.8	13.4	Finish Job
14.5	11.5	15.4	15.8	Quality
10.7	10.1	12.2	12.9	Affect
10.9	11.0	11.6	13.6	Empathy
12.4	14.7	12.6	10.5	Sociability
11.9	12.4	11.9	10.5	Loyalty
16.0	14.2	12.6	11.2	Dominance
13.8	13.8	9.8	11.0	Status
13.4	15.3	10.0	8.0	Politics
11.6	11.6	14.9	14.1	Leadership
9.9	10.4	12.2	13.4	Abstraction
12.1	12.2	15.4	15.6	Detail/Organization
8.7	12.6	9.2	12.6	Exposition
12.3	11.6	12.7	12.6	Flexibility
.35	.31	.40	.36	Mean Intercorrelation

politicized environments, membership in different factions and coalitions rather than effort or competence plays a primary role in the distribution of rewards. Therefore, one's knowledge of and connection to groups—in-a-word, one's sociability—is very important. Similarly, fluency of expression and command of argument, that is—exposition—is highly valued. The presence of these three factors simultaneously is a very sure indicator that your culture is dysfunctionally political.

Culture Strength of Units A and B. To assess the strength of the two units' cultures, we refer to the numbers at the bottom of the four columns labeled mean intercorrelation. (The companion disk to this book contains a program that computes this and other statistics. The CVAT program calculates it automatically.) Without recourse to complex math, we can say that the mean intercorrelation is a measure of how similar our sample's responses are one to another. An intercorrelation of 1 means that everyone in the sample proffered 100 percent identical responses. This never happens, although I have seen correlations as high as .90 in some religious sects. A correlation of 0 indicates that everyone answered the survey differently from everyone else. This also almost never happens.

Given our definition of culture strength as homogeneity of behavior and thought, it stands to reason that organizations in which there is substantial agreement about desired values have stronger cultures than those with less agreement. I therefore use the mean intercorrelation as an approximate measure of culture strength. Experience suggests that a business organization with a correlation of .15 or less on the descriptive profile has a weak culture. A correlation of .45 or greater is indicative of a rather strong culture. Values above .60 are rare and indicate very strong culture. (Ideal values are usually more homogeneous; between .30 and .70 are common.)

Unit A has only a slightly higher mean intercorrelation than B for both real (.35 versus .31) and ideal (.40 versus .36) profiles, suggesting that for this case at least, culture content is more important than strength in determining the performance differences observed. Up to a point, this is typical of other situations I have seen: culture content is usually much more important for predicting performance and identifying problems than is culture strength.

There are, however, a couple of caveats worth noting. When the strength of an organization's culture is at least moderate (above .25 mean intercorrelation), its content seems to be the determining factor in performance. However, extremely weak cultures (as indicated by the mean intercorrelation) appear unable to homogenize people's thought or behavior to the point where the content of the culture has any impact on performance at all. In my experience, very weak cultures are never associated with high performance. When they do not have dysfunctional content, they often appear to have little content at all—illustrated by few peaks and valleys in the profile. The firm with the flattest CVAT profile I ever saw went out of business three months after data were collected. With few exceptions, I would consider a mean intercorrelation under .15 as highly problematic, especially if the content is questionable.

A second caveat regards very strong cultures. They tend to be associated either very good or very poor performance, and they are almost always accompanied quite distinctive content. The consulting firm I described earlier was one of these. Consider the CVAT data in Table 4.7.

Note both the high mean intercorrelation and the extreme values in the work and affect quadrants. These numbers indicate a very strong and vital but unbalanced culture. Given the great work motivation and agility that this culture probably inculcates in its members, the rapid rise of this firm is understandable. Whether this same pressure-cooker culture can sustain performance over time or whether it will implode is another question.

Summarizing the discussion above, we can provide some possible answers for our four questions about ideal culture content and strength. Strong political emphasis in the content of a culture (as indicated by the

Table 4.7 Profile of Pressure Cooker Consulting Ltd.

15.7	Effort
14.5	Time
16.1	Finish Job
15.4	Quality
7.7	Affect
6.8	Empathy
8.5	Sociability
11.5	Loyalty
13.6	Dominance
14.5	Status
14.5	Politics
12.1	Leadership
11.8	Abstraction
11.4	Detail/Organization
12.9	Exposition
13.0	Flexibility
.55	Mean Intercorrelation

"real" profile) is almost always bad news, high emphasis on quality and effort is almost always good news; high politics, sociability, and exposition together are symptomatic of serious politicization. Very weak cultures are usually undesirable; cultures of moderate strength can favor or disfavor performance depending on their content; and very strong cultures are usually very high performing or very pathological.

Other Ways of Getting At Ideal Culture

Hopefully, the restaurant cases have stimulated some thought about ideal culture strength and content, but they have obviously not exhausted the subject. I now pursue some other approaches. One logical response to question 1 (What culture content is best for our organization?) is merely to take the mean ideal profile of everyone in the organization. It is democratic and intuitive and would seem to be an efficient way of arriving at a cultural consensus. By the same token, it would seem logical to simply take the difference between the ideal and real profiles to measure the health of a culture. Indeed, the high performing restaurant A features less distance between ideal and real than unit B on seven dimensions. Moreover, the fact that both units are very close on many ideal values shows that the employees' view of the ideal culture is largely unaltered by the differing climates reflected by the descriptive (real) profiles.

Drawbacks of the Ideal ProFile

The real-ideal approach has merit, and it is a very efficient yet comprehensive way to get a bearing on a culture. However, one should not uncritically assume that employee satisfaction with a culture means that the culture is perfect, or that the ideal culture is perfectly defined by the sum of employee aspirations. Our appliance manufacturer case points up one reason why this may not be so, and other reasons become apparent with some thought.

The strong relationship between the CEO and VP-HR's personal values and their ideal culture illustrates how business needs are not the sole determinant of corporate culture. Personal preferences, departmental and professional loyalties, and other factors also enter in. It is also true that what employees want their organization to value is not identical to what customers or other stakeholders would like to see.

A second problem stems from the possibility that average scores may mask important internal divisions in the firm. In Chapter 2, we discussed the tendency of social systems toward reciprocal opposition and polarization. Organizational cultures are not immune to these proclivities. In fact, I believe that culture is one of the properties of organizations where reciprocal opposition first becomes apparent. If one of the oppositional groups favors loyalty in the organization, it is likely that the other will consider it unimportant. If the size of the groups is similar, this will lead to situations where scores will cancel each other out—that is, one group uniformly scores loyalty at 18, the other at 8, leaving a mean of 13. We may thus be erroneously led to believe that loyalty is of minor importance to the content of the culture, when in fact it is a burning issue.

A third problem has its origins in one of the great dilemmas of organizational culture: the stronger a culture is, the less visible it is to insiders, and the more it impedes the entrance of information from outside. It assumes a taken-for-grantedness that is hard to overcome. For instance, in organizations that are highly politically oriented, people come to perceive office politics as normal and therefore are unlikely to think of political behavior as abnormal, and equally unlikely to think of ways of acting that are less political. Their descriptive profiles are likely to underestimate the importance of politics in the organization and even the desired profile may show little need for change. Because strong cultures mean less permeable boundaries, external information identifying the politicized nature of the organization is likely to be denied or filtered out.

These problems do not mean that real and ideal profiles should not be used, but they do call for additional analyses to avoid biases and uncover hidden dysfunctions. I will propose two, an external sample and CONCOR analysis.

External Samples

The logic of an external sample is simple. If the culture is blinding employees to the true values of the organization, a small sample of outsiders who know the organization well should provide an independent perspective. The external sample also speaks to disjunctures between employee and client preferences, and it may also ameliorate problems arising from linkages between personal and collective values.

The appliance company discussed earlier in this chapter took an external sample for these very reasons. The results are found in Table 4.8.

One of the largest differences, and probably the most important, is flexibility. Stakeholders want considerably more flexibility in the firm than do employees. Stakeholders also appear to tolerate less empathy and favor more control generally, especially leadership. Given the natural tendency for employees in a company to favor more empathy and less control, the stakeholders' perspective may offer a more objective view of the ideal culture on these dimensions. In any event, stakeholder perceptions can be used as a check against the preferences of employees.

CONCOR Analysis of Ideal Cultures

As I mentioned above, people do not always agree about the ideal content of a culture, just as they may not agree in their descriptions of the real culture of an enterprise. One should not automatically assume that the mathematical average of all members of an organization on a given dimension represents a consensus about what should be done. Sometimes the mean is no more than an amalgamation of radically different opinions, particularly in situations that are polarized or factionalized. For instance, if you took a poll on the desirability of private property in Russia during the early 1900s you would probably get a mean of about 5.5 on a scale of 10. This result would appear to mean that Russians held moderate opinions about private property. In reality, of course, half the population was 10s and the other half was 1s.

To avoid this problem, a mechanism of identifying the location and strength of divergent opinion is needed. One common and very inefficient way is to divide up your sample using criteria like hierarchical level, department, or seniority, that might be expected to cause differences in opinion. This approach, which by the way is the foundation for almost all attitudinal research in management, has two problems. First, it can take forever to analyze all of the possible criteria, most of which will have small or trivial effects. Second, groupings of different opinions are almost never caused by just one or two variables. Rather, they come about through a combination of factors and historical processes. More often than not, clusters of different opinions are reflective of the different social groups that we discussed earlier.

Table 4.8   Ideal Cultures of Employees Versus External Stakeholders

External	Internal	
12.2	13.5	Effort
12.8	12.2	Time
14.9	14.2	Finish Job
15.9	15.5	Quality
10.4	11.9	Affect
12.4	14.6	Empathy
14.0	13.5	Sociability
15.3	14.9	Loyalty
10.4	8.8	Dominance
12.4	7.6	Status
14.0	8.8	Politics
15.3	13.0	Leadership
13.3	13.0	Detail/Organization
10.9	11.3	Exposition
15.0	13.3	Flexibility

For this reason, the most effective way to approach the problem of diverse opinions in the organization is to first locate clusters of such opinions, then look at the attributes of the people making up these clusters. Locating clusters is quite easy thanks to any number of mathematical algorithms developed by academics with nothing better to do.

The Convergence of Iterated Correlations (CONCOR) (Breiger et al. 1975) algorithm included in the companion disk for this book was developed by sociologists at Harvard and is commonly used in analyzing social networks (see Chapter 5). However, I have also found it quite useful for locating clusters of people with similar opinions. CONCOR works by comparing each respondent's scores on all sixteen CVAT dimensions with every other person's scores. CONCOR makes two groups of the most similar responses initially, and then, if you tell it to, it can split each of those groups into two as long as you have people to divide up. If you don't like my CVAT or culture matrix dimensions, you can use your own; the algorithm doesn't care what the numbers mean as long as it has a string of numbers of the same length for each person.

Once CONCOR has divided up the sample (two groups is usually sufficient), one looks at the differences between means to find out whether the culture is polarized and on what dimensions. Small differences are not a matter for great concern. One should expect some differences, because CONCOR is very good at locating any differences that exist. After ascertaining the magnitude and type of differences, it is good to look at the composition of the CONCOR groups to see if there are any regularities in personal attributes or organizational status. This will help one to understand the origins of disparate values, and in all likelihood will lead to the important social groups in the organization.

A Bank Merger

Consider the case below of a small regional bank that acquired a failing competitor. I was called in three years after the merger to see how the culture was doing generally, and specifically to see if the parent and acquired branches were heading in the same direction culturally. One of my first moves was of course to compare real and ideal profiles for the entire organization, as shown in Table 4.9.

Overall, the profile looks good. The all-important dimensions of politics, sociability, and exposition are comparatively low, and there is not too much distance between the real and the ideal in these areas. Leadership and quality dimensions are high and close to the ideal. The areas that raise some concern are effort and loyalty. People would like more of both dimensions; and, as one might suspect, employees from the acquired branches perceive the company as being much less loyalty-oriented than those of the original parent (acquired = 10.0, parent = 13.9).

The CONCOR split (or partition) of the Ideal culture does not contradict this rosy picture, but it does add significant information that is worth some attention.

Note that one group, the smaller of the two, favors a much more cerebral organization: 15.7 versus 12.1 in abstraction, 15.2 versus 12.7 in organization, 12.4 versus 10.2 in exposition, and 13.7 versus 10.3 in flexibility. Group 1 is willing to sacrifice leadership, loyalty, and above all effort, to have its more intellectual organization. Clearly a minority, one wonders who these thirteen intellectuals out of thirty-eight employees might be. I did a quick review of various attributes of members of this grouping and found that only three of the thirteen come from the acquired branches, but more than half (seven) are officers of the bank. Group two, with twenty-five members, contains only six bank officers. Clearly part of the management of the bank wants to take the employees somewhere they do not want to go culturally. If they choose to try, they have quite a selling job in front of them, with both acquired and original staff.

Although the differences in ideal culture that we find in the CONCOR groupings of our bank case are cause for some concern and consensus building, they are minor compared to what I found in analyzing CONCOR groupings for the appliance factory.

Changing Cultures

I cannot stress enough the need for careful diagnosis before intervening in a culture. A good diagnosis will tell how strong the culture is, which aspects

Table 4.9 Cultural Profiles of Bank, Three Years Post Merger

Real	Ideal	
13.8	16.3	Effort
12.2	12.8	Time
12.2	12.5	Finish Job
17.4	16.5	Quality
11.3	12.6	Affect
9.4	10.7	Empathy
12.8	11.1	Sociability
12.9	14.7	Loyalty
13.3	12.2	Dominance
11.5	9.8	Status
9.9	7.4	Politics
14.9	14.8	Leadership
13.2	13.3	Abstraction
11.8	13.6	Detail/Organization
11.5	10.9	Exposition
12.5	11.4	Flexibility

are desirable, which need change, and how difficult change will be. Moreover, if one has also diagnosed the environment, goals, activity system, and other boundaries, one may conclude that a strong culture is not essential, in which case much needless effort is saved by being satisfied with somewhat weaker values.

After completing a careful diagnosis and ascertaining what values would be best for the organization, one faces what I call the fix-or-start-over question. As the reader may suspect by now, a strong culture can be very hard to change. Because strong cultures tend to be taken for granted and are therefore invisible, they can be quite recalcitrant. Like teaching a tone-deaf person to sing, unteaching people things that they have come to take for granted can be almost hopeless. Also, because culture takes a long time to develop and is both an expression of individual values and an influence upon them, changes in strong cultures collide with individual values and identities in a very volatile way.

Four Options

For these reasons, if a culture is very strong and very undesirable, it is better to tear it down and start over. Even eradicating the old culture will be difficult, though, and building a new one on the habits and expectations of the old one is a big job. If a culture is strong and desirable, it will be worth trying to fix those things that don't work while keeping most values intact.

If a culture is weak and undesirable, it will be relatively easy to eradicate; but one will have to start from scratch in building a new one, and that will take work. Finally, if a culture is weak and desirable, you will want to strengthen and update it. Figure 4.3 summarizes these four options and their comparative difficulty:

In contemplating whether to buy or liquidate an existing company, the figure above has clear implications (Gopalan et al. 1994). A strong dysfunctional culture creates a number of very real financial and psychological liabilities. Unless the business is a real gold mine, it won't be worth it. Consider instead just purchasing the physical assets if they can be had cheaply. Alternatively, if you wait awhile, the firm will probably fold and you can save some money. On the other hand, a firm with a strong healthy culture can be a bargain even if it is distressed financially, especially if its values are similar to those the would-be buyer espouses personally. Below I discuss some of the change strategies that go with each of the four options.

Change Strategies for the Four Scenarios

Strengthening a Weak Functional Culture or Maintaining a Strong Functional Culture

Of the four possibilities, strengthening a weak functional culture and maintaining a strong functional culture are easiest. If a culture is weak but functional, one will need to do little to change the content of the culture (the hardest task). Instead, one simply cultivates what is already there. And if a culture is strong and functional, one need only maintain it. Still, as is the case with buildings and relationships, it is much harder to maintain or strengthen a culture than to weaken it. The key to either strengthening/ maintaining or weakening a culture lies in understanding those forces that create cultures in the first place, or what Wilkins and Ouchi (1983) call the preconditions for the development of organizational culture. They are:

1. Long and stable history
2. Absence of institutional alternatives
3. Interaction between members
4. High transaction costs

Long, Stable History. To strengthen a culture, stability is paramount. One should avoid wild swings in strategy and tactics, and develop a strong organizational memory through traditions and commemorative events. Try to develop trust between employees, managers, and clients, and keep turnover to a bare minimum. Of course, nothing can be done to increase

Figure 4.3   Organization Culture Change Strategies

	Weak	Strong
Undesirable	1 Eradicate (Easy)	2 Eradicate (Very Hard)
Desirable	3 Build (Hard)	4 Maintain/Enhance (Easy)

the age of the organization, but the above suggestions can insure that any history it does have is venerable.

Absence of Institutional Alternatives.   Much could be said about absence of institutional alternatives, but in a nutshell it means that one doesn't do business in the same way that one's competitors do. Also, low-institutional-alternative organizations tend to train their people from the ground up rather than hiring experienced people from competitors. In general, contact with other industry players is minimal. This isolation leads to unique values and perspectives and can be the basis of a strong culture. Some organizations, like police departments and the old Bell system, have no direct competitors; and for this reason they develop very strong cultures. Organizations that are not in such an advantaged position will need to take a fundamentally different approach to the market to develop a truly strong culture. If they develop some unique competence or approach that sets them apart, their customers and employees will soon pick up on it. Even minor actions that communicate this difference can have an impact. For instance, a restaurant could be the only burger joint in town where the servers wear bow ties. A beauty shop could be the only hairdresser with private booths. A religious congregation could be the only church in town that takes videotapes of services to shut-ins. Such distinctive actions communicate unique values, which in turn contribute to culture strength.

High Transaction Costs.   Like institutional alternatives, defining and explaining transaction costs could take up many pages, but for practical use, the concept can be expressed simply. Organizations with high transaction costs look at more than just an individual's raw output in assessing and rewarding performance. Instead they evaluate the whole individual over time, paying a substantial, predictable salary rather than commissions or hourly wages. Bonuses are often determined by group or organizational performance rather than individual output. This type of reward system tends to give the employee a longer-term orientation and a broader view of his or her role in the organization, making it easier to assimilate desired values. In the short run, this can be expensive, but for certain businesses it helps to create a unique atmosphere and foster better service.

Interaction Between Members.   Frequent interaction between members of an organization is absolutely necessary for a strong culture to develop. Cultures are not generally transmitted by rules, manuals, memos, or other formal means. They develop more easily when people associate with other people on a face-to-face basis. Interaction between members communicates subtle behavioral cues, expectations, role models, stories, and other intangibles that communicate essential values. Strong-culture firms arrange their physical space and social agendas to foster contact between members.

Weakening Dysfunctional Cultures

To eradicate a culture, as in scenarios 1 and 2 above, simply erode the four preconditions for the development of culture. This is much easier than building a culture. A short and highly varied history with lots of changes, high turnover, and no traditions is easier to achieve than stability. Business carried out using standard industry practices with little uniqueness and deviation from the norms requires only careful observation and faithful imitation. Hiring a substantial proportion of employees who have worked for competitors should be easy and helps in replicating standard industry practices. Preventing interaction between employees beyond that necessary to formally accomplish their jobs can be done easily by staggering lunch hours, physical isolation, and other means. For many jobs, pay can be based solely on measurable output with no thought for other considerations.

While this state of affairs may not make for a particularly beloved workplace or produce a unique image, this cultureless state is better than a dysfunctional culture. It can even serve as a viable, long-term setup for firms that provide basic products and services to a stable, cost-sensitive market. Backyard Enterprises, discussed in Chapter 1, is archetypical of a business that not only can do without a strong culture, it cannot afford the added high transaction costs, stability, and uniqueness that strong cultures require. If a domain is narrow and stable, boundaries are permeable, the activity system is complex, and costs are low, little or no culture may be best. Routine management techniques may offer all the control needed. Again, the key is to have everything that is necessary and nothing that is not.

For organizations with strong or weak dysfunctional cultures, the cultureless organization can be a necessary temporary state or even a long-term alternative before trying to build a new culture. This rather sterile environment gives people time to distance themselves from the emotions and limitations of the old culture and break away from old rules and practices. By minimizing the preconditions for culture and establishing clear, concise managerial controls that stipulate desired performance and administer rewards and punishments fairly, many businesses can function quite efficiently for long periods. Gradually, this more bureaucratic organization can be relaxed as a suitable culture is developed.

Influencing Culture Content

Of all the options suggested, the greatest challenge is influencing culture content. Making fundamental changes in the content of a strong culture is rarely worth the effort. It is like remodeling a Victorian house to look like a ranch style—you're better off tearing it down and starting over. That is why dysfunctional cultures are best eradicated and followed by a period of sterile, bureaucratic management. However, weak or strong cultures that require redirection on just one or two dimensions can be successfully altered; and new cultures can be created from scratch.

The key to culture content, I believe, is to create a stream of concrete managerial actions that express the desired values both symbolically and organizationally. At Nissan, for instance, the CEO felt the need for a more egalitarian and less inward-looking culture. Among specific measures taken were removal of rank from identification badges and issuing of competitors' cars to top executives. Non-ranked name badges meant there is no immediate way of knowing where an employee stands in the hierarchy so that other criteria become more prominent in the relationship. Use of competitor vehicles forced an acquaintance with developments in the industry and signaled the importance of being aware of competitors' moves. These moves in themselves were not revolutionary; but they were accompanied by a flood of other measures with similar messages. Plants were given much more discretion over budgets, a new organization structure was market-rather than production-based, new car engineering was decentralized, younger managers were promoted, and complaint desks were set up in dealerships. Together, these acts created a new understanding of what the company valued and ultimately led to much-improved financial performance (Kotter and Heskett 1992).

My personal experience feeding CVAT data back to clients underscores the importance of concrete actions in determining people's perceptions of corporate culture. Invariably when I ask members of feedback groups why a given dimension has a particularly high or low score, they respond with stories of actual events—often happenings with rather trivial practical consequences but pregnant with symbolism. To illustrate how important status is to the organization they'll tell about how the cleaning staff has been instructed to clean the president's office first. They'll tell how an employee was forced to borrow the HR manager's tie before an appointment with the CEO. To illustrate the inability to complete tasks, they'll relate that it took a four-hour meeting to decide what color the new carpeting should be. They'll recall how the plant manager periodically checks the restrooms for slackers.

Selective Disdain

Stories about "piddly stuff" have enormous power to signal organizational values, and managers should be aware of the symbolic importance of even the most trivial acts. In influencing culture content, though, there is an important reason to search for actions that have both symbolic and substantive value. I call it the "selective rejection" or "selective disdain" principle. If management formally espouses a value, minor or symbolic actions that are consistent with this value tend to be seen as ritualisms or tokenisms. On the other hand, minor actions that management takes which are inconsistent with these values will be seen as a genuine expression of the organization's true colors.

For this reason, a large number of both symbolic and substantive actions are required to give credibility to formal organizational values. This is also the reason why the best actions are those that carry both symbolic meaning and practical implications, like promotions and structural changes. For this reason also, it is probably best to frame a mission or value statement after a culture has taken hold rather than before.

There are other ways to influence culture content. As we have already suggested, one of the most potent is the selection of employees with personal values that match the desired culture content. Another is the use of vocabulary and categories (remember the case of the accounting company made up of "gentlemen") that are consistent with desired values. The repetition of special events and folklore can also be a potent force. But the most direct and effective way to influence a culture's content is by making sure that management decisions and actions reflect and embody the espoused values. In this regard, organization cultures are like children. They will faithfully disregard everything that is said, but they pick up immediately on the meaning of every concrete act.

5

Seeing the Invisible Activity System: Social Networks in Organizations

In Chapter 1 we discussed the activity system—defined as a predictable way of doing the organization's work—as one of three principal components of any organization. In Chapter 2, among other things, we talked about some of the ways activity systems get out of wack. Included as activity system dysfunctions were blocked flows, irrelevant content, and high and low density. Other dysfunctions, such as frivolous complexity and dualisms, can show up in a number of places, but they are often located in the activity system or influence it.

In this chapter we take up the activity system again but in a very specific way. Earlier we focused on flows—the movement of inputs through the system on their way to becoming outputs. Here we will examine the arrangement or configuration of individuals in the organization and the ties or contacts that connect them. Traditionally this has been defined as organization structure, and at least a generation of scholars have conducted arcane, painstaking research trying to understand and optimize it. Unfortunately, much of this work has been carried out in large corporations and public bureaucracies and is so esoteric as to be of little relevance for practicing managers, even in large organizations. For the manager of smaller or nontraditional organizations, it has very limited value.

This does not mean, however, that structure is not important in all organizations. It is a critical part of the activity system and merits theattention of the managers of the smallest businesses. This chapter aims to make the structure accessible to and diagnosable by practitioners using the concept of network analysis or sociometry—an old technique which has only relatively recently been used for figuring out organization structure. The bulk of this chapter will concern itself with explaining and applying social network analysis in a way that normal people can understand and use. Before I do this however, I will review the two major traditional approaches to organization structure and their limitations.

Traditional Approaches to Organization Structure

Organization Charts

Historically, there have been two ways of looking at organization structure. The one most commonly used by managers and consultants is the venerable organization chart. Organization charts are essentially little maps of formal relationships in which boxes represent people or departments, and lines indicate who reports to whom. (There are no arrows on the lines indicating who reports to whom, but it is historically assumed that those lower on the page report to those above them.) People or departments typically have titles attached to them that give an indication of their general function in the organization.

Since its invention some one hundred years ago, the organization chart has proven an indispensable means of thinking about structure, communicating changes, signaling power, identifying responsibilities, and generally disseminating an official version of the organization. Of course, it has always been known that organization charts don't tell the whole story—they are incomplete maps at best, and sometimes quite misleading. A number of limitations can be cited.

Limitations to Organization Charts.   First, there are many more relationships in the organization, both in type and number, than are portrayed in the organization chart. Organization charts or organograms (as Henry Mintzberg, 1979, likes to call them) record mostly formal reporting relationships which delineate responsibility and authority. They do not indicate how frequently superiors and subordinates interact, or whether peers interact at all, yet considerable research as well as common sense suggests that frequency of interaction has a major impact on how we behave toward other people (Homans 1950; Organ and Bateman 1992). They do not indicate committee memberships, or who depends on whom for important information, or who collaborating with whom on special projects, or who possesses important resources because of his or her central position in the work flow. All of these are important to the way organizations function.

Organization charts do not tell us about the informal organization consisting of friendships, dislikes, alliances, coalitions, the ascendant and declining fortunes of managers occupying the same hierarchical level, and a dozen other quirky elements. Yet every manager has stories to tell of situations where the informal organization bears little relation to the formal chart and is much more important for getting things done.

Organization charts have a built-in hierarchical bias, unequivocally placing one person over another and establishing an inviolable chain of command. This may be fine if the organization wants to promote a rigid, pyramid-like structure: but many organizations are currently seeking more fluid, egalitarian forms that downplay hierarchy, rigid division of labor, and territorial boundaries (Wheatly 1992). For such firms, the exclusive use of a traditional organization chart may send the wrong message.

These limitations to the traditional organization chart are particularly problematic for smaller organizations. The relative informality of smaller organizations means that it is particularly important for managers to have an accurate depiction of the social texture of the firm, and of course a traditional organizational chart cannot provide this. The smaller number of people means that it is both possible and important that management have a grasp of who is communicating with whom, whether formal reporting relationships are being honored, and whether cliques or factions are developing.

In the smaller organization the division of labor is rarely so minute that one person has only one function, so an understanding of positions in the small organization is much more dependent on a knowledge of actual relationships than is the case in larger organizations. A chart that tells us that so-and-so is the VP of operations or marketing director tells us little about how he or she fits into the activity system of a small organization. Other problems could be cited, but the basic point has been made—there is much that managers in smaller organizations need to know about social structure that cannot be found on the organization chart.

The Dimensional Approach

The second way of looking at organization structure can be called the dimensional approach (Hall 1976). It is used mostly by researchers and academics, although most managers and consultants use the concepts either implicitly or explicitly. The dimensional view of organization structure involves identifying and measuring abstract properties of the relationships and procedures that make up organizations. For instance, span of control, a common dimension used to measure structure, deals with the number of subordinate relations a manager entertains. Vertical differentiation, or height, refers to the number of intermediary relationships separating the top of the organization from the bottom. Formalization considers the number of rules and written records used to regulate work. It also deals with the flows of information, resources, and commands between people and units in the organization. Centralization refers to the extent to which decision privileges converge on progressively fewer individuals. Horizontal differentiation deals with the degree to which responsibilities are subdivided in the firm.

Together, these dimensions provide a feel for the overall character of the entire organization. An organization with few layers, little formalization, and long span of control for instance, will behave in a very different fashion from one with many layers, much formalization and a short span of control. The dimensions are precise and easily measured and, unlike organization charts, they can be standardized for comparison across organizations. Researchers have conducted extensive studies on what technical, environmental, and strategic conditions match different configurations of dimensions: thus the dimensional approach offers general guidelines on how to best structure organizations for given business conditions.

Limitations to the Dimensional Approach.   Obviously, the dimensional approach has its limitations, too. The general maxims about structure, strategy, and environment that academics have worked out with such care are usually too generic to apply to specific situations. For instance, the oft-cited observation that mass-production firms should have more minute division of labor and longer span of control than other types of production (Woodward 1965) does not tell us how jobs should be divided up, or what jobs should report to which managers, or which rules should be used in formalizing behaviors.

Again, as is the case with organization charts, the informal organization is left behind. Measures of centralization, span, number of layers, and the like often do not tell us how frequently managers interact with their subordinates, which VPs are most influential, or how often subordinates interact directly with top management rather than going through channels. Some very elaborate organization designs are largely ignored or subverted by employees, while others are followed to the letter. Conversely, the informal and formal processes of some rather lean organization designs are sometimes very close and at other times very distant.

The dimensional approach is probably even less useful for small organizations than the organization chart approach. The smaller the organization, the fewer the layers and the less meaningful they are. The same applies for other dimensions—fewer narrowly-defined positions, fewer uses for formalization, shorter spans of control, and so on. As a result, the masses of research matching formal structural dimensions with environmental and strategic types give the manager of the small organization very little in the way of concrete practical advice.

A More Recent Approach: Network Analysis

In recent years a growing number of researchers have turned to sociometry—a body of techniques for mapping social relationships—as a tool for understanding organizations. Because sociometry—or social network analysis, as it is more broadly termed—looks directly at the actual ties or relationships that make up organization structure, it avoids several of the disadvantages of the traditional approaches described above. It also features several advantages, particularly for those in smaller or nontraditional organizations who need an accurate and detailed view of how the organization really works and stand to gain little by agonizing over the composition of a formal organization chart.

Unfortunately, network analysts' proclivity for complex mathematics and even more complex social theory has kept it out of the reach of most practitioners. This need not be so, however; basic sociometric techniques can easily be grasped and applied to many practical situations without the grounding in mathematical esoterica enjoyed by the leading academics.

I will now explain the rudiments of network analysis applied to organizations, catalogue its advantages over traditional approaches to organization structure, and use examples from my own experience to illustrate how network analysis can be used to diagnose organizations. As was the case with the material on organizational culture, the companion disk to this volume can be used for network analysis (contact author for details).

A Network Primer

The utility of network analysis for understanding and diagnosing organization structure is more easily explained after the reader has a basic understanding of sociometric technique. The approach I present here, called blockmodelling (White et al. 1976) is one of the more easily accessible techniques. I will illustrate it using an organization chart and network data from the top two management layers of one of my clients, a diversified manufacturing company with about eight thousand employees.

I recognize that a firm with eight thousand is larger than those inhabited by most of my readers, so I will restrict myself to the very top layers of the firm, which include only ten people and feature the same informality found in basic work units and small business. A more complete discussion of these data can be found in Nelson (1990), and portions of that article are reproduced verbatim here.

Networks Defined

A social network is defined as a set of ties (or contacts) that link individuals or groups (sometimes called actors). Many different kinds of relationships may make up a network—friendship ties, information exchange, dependence, approval requests, or others. Network analysts usually study one kind of contact at a time or use frequency of contact as a general measure of the strength of a relationship. In my own experience I have found that three aspects of relationships capture much of what goes on in organizations—frequency of contact, degree of dependence, and frequency of formal approval requests.

Frequency of contact is a good surrogate for the intensity and intimacy of the relationship; people in very frequent contact tend to become friends or enemies, usually the former (Granovetter 1973). Dependency tells how much informal power a person can leverage by controlling things needed by others. Approval requests are indicative of how often a given person exercises formal authority over another. Consider now the organization chart in Figure 5.1, which expresses principally the third kind of relationship:

Although this chart shares all of the weaknesses related above, it does tell us a number of important things about the organization. We know that this is a multidivisional firm with at least six business units and ten executives at the general-manager level or above. Two divisional managers (Heavy Products and Tiny Products) report directly to the CEO, one division (strangely) reports to the VP for Human Resources, and three are subordinate to another vice president. Human Resources and Finance are the only staff functions with their own vice presidents.

In all, this organization chart identifies nine formal ties or relationships, three to the VP of Light Products, five to the CEO, and one to the VP for Human Resources. Of course, the number of possible contacts of one type between the ten individuals above is much greater—ten squared minus ten,

Figure 5.1   Organization Chart of Multidivisional Firm

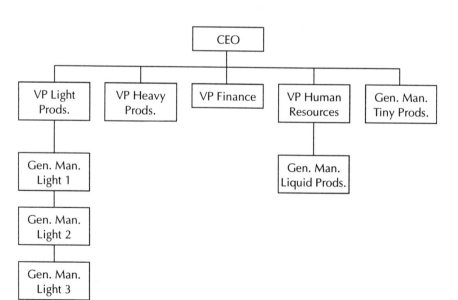

or ninety, if we assume that ties need not be reciprocal. For instance, one subordinate may depend on the other, but not vice versa: or both can be mutually dependent, so there would be ninety dependence ties if everyone were dependent on everyone else.

I collected data about the average weekly frequency of contact, degree of dependence, and number of formal approval requests in an average month for the executives above, but in order to keep this demonstration simple, I will discuss only the formal approval requests—the type of relationship closest to information used as the basis of traditional organizational charts.

What to Ask

Data collection is quite simple. One simply provides each manager a list of all other managers along with instructions to supply information about the number and type of each relationship being studied (in this case, formal approval requests):

Approvals	
1. CEO	_____
2. VP Light Products	_____
3. VP Heavy Products	_____
4. VP Finance	_____
5. VP Human Resources	_____
6. GM Tiny Products	_____
7. GM Liquid Products	_____
8. GM Light Prods. 1	_____
9. GM Lights Prods. 2	_____
10. GM Light Prods. 3	_____

"How many times in an average month do you ask the persons below for some kind of official approval? (Examples: expenditure authorizations, budget approvals, overtime requests, scheduling changes, etc.)"

When the questionnaires are returned, each individual questionnaire becomes a row in a 10 by 10 matrix, called a sociomatrix or adjacency matrix. The responses of our ten managers regarding approval requests are given in Table 5.2.

What Is Really Going on Here

If we carefully examine this matrix, it becomes clear that the formal organization chart tells us some things but does not reveal others. As the chart

Table 5.1   Adjacency Matrix of Multidivisional Firm

	1	2	3	4	5	6	7	8	9	10
1. CEO	×	0	0	0	0	0	0	0	0	0
2. VP Light Products	10	×	0	8	5	0	0	0	0	0
3. VP Heavy Products	20	0	×	2	3	0	0	0	0	0
4. VP Finance	5	0	0	×	10	0	0	0	0	0
5. VP H. R.	0	0	0	0	×	0	0	0	0	0
6. GM Tiny Products	1	0	0	0	2	×	0	0	0	0
7. GM Liquid Products	2	0	0	0	2	0	×	0	0	0
8. GM Light Prods. 1	0	2	0	0	0	0	0	×	0	0
9 GM Light Prods. 2	0	4	0	0	0	0	0	0	×	0
10. GM Light Prods. 3	0	2	0	0	0	0	0	0	0	×
Column Sums	38	8	0	10	22	0	0	0	0	0

suggests, Light Managers 1, 2, and 3 make approval requests of the VP of Light Products and no one else. Observing the network of the VP of Human Resources, however, we see that the organization chart does not tell the whole story. Summing columns to find out who receives most approval requests, we note that the VP of Human Resources is second only to the CEO in requests received (twenty-two versus thirty-eight for the CEO), and yet he does not make any approval requests. Indeed, the VP of Human Resources receives approval requests from virtually the same people who make approval requests to the CEO. In network terms we say that the VP/HR is structurally equivalent to the CEO.

My personal knowledge of this organization confirms that, as the adjacency matrix suggests, the VP of Human Resources is indeed very influential. He is, in fact, second in command in this organization and has formal and informal responsibilities that go far beyond the traditional personnel function. An astute observer studying the organization chart might sense something out of the ordinary upon noting that Human Resources has formal line responsibility for one of the company's operations—quite rare for the personnel function. However, the adjacency matrix tells a much more complete story.

Other insights come from the adjacency matrix. Note that GM Tiny Products and GM Liquids make approval requests to both the CEO and the VP of Human Resources, while other general managers make requests only to VP Light Products. This suggests (accurately so) that Tiny Products and Liquids are higher-status divisions than Light 1, 2, and 3. This is clear from

Tiny Product's direct report to the CEO on the formal organization chart, but Liquid's status is only ascertained from the adjacency matrix.

Most of the information contained in our adjacency matrix example is common knowledge to the insiders in the organization, albeit not in such precise terms. However, if we were to descend another two levels in this organization to the middle management region, the network becomes so large that we face the problem of pluralistic ignorance. That is, any individual knows who composes her individual network and how it functions, but no one individual has sufficient contacts to understand the entire network. This is one reason why things "fall through the cracks" when organizations get more than fifteen or twenty employees; noone is able to accurately view the entire network. However, by collecting network data every now and then, an exhaustive, precise view or the entire organization can be had at a glance. And that information, we will see later, can help spot a number of problems that would otherwise be invisible.

Mapping Larger Networks: Density Tables and Blockmodels

As the matrix becomes larger it ultimately becomes very difficult to pay close attention to individual networks, and some way to simplify the raw matrix is necessary. To do this, we use the abovementioned principle of structural equivalence. People with similar networks are placed into groups or blocks which can then be compared to one another. The CONCOR computer program included on your disk does this quickly and easily, but in the case above, you can see which networks are similar just by looking at the rows and columns of the matrix.

Clearly the CEO and VP of Human Resources belong together, as do general managers of Light divisions 1, 2, and 3. The networks of the general managers of Tiny and Liquid Products are also very similar. VP Light Products and VP Heavy Products are similar, except for VP Light's three subordinates. The VP of Finance is not similar to anyone, but the closest grouping would be with general managers Tiny and Liquids. If we permute (rearrange) the columns and rows of the matrix above according to the groupings proposed, it is possible to capture the essence of the network structure in a simple representation. Table 5.2 is the permuted adjacency matrix.

The essential features of this matrix can be summarized in a density table. The number of contacts in a region is divided by the area or number of possible relationships. Thus, the density of the first region (CEO and VP Human Resources × CEO × VP Human Resources) is 0 divided by 2 or 0. The density of approval requests from the second group (VP Finance, GM Tiny, and GM Liquids) to the first (CEO and VP Human Resources) is about 3.67, or 22 divided by 6. Once all of these divisions are done, we get a density table that looks like Table 5.3.

Table 5.2   Permuted Adjacency Matrix

	1	5	4	6	7	2	3	8	9	10
1. CEO	×	0	0	0	0	0	0	0	0	0
2. VP Light Products	0	×	0	0	0	0	0	0	0	0
3. VP Heavy Products	5	10	×	0	0	0	0	0	0	0
4. VP Finance	1	2	0	×	0	0	0	0	0	0
5. VP H. R.	2	2	0	0	×	0	0	0	0	0
6. GM Tiny Products	10	5	8	0	0	×	0	0	0	0
7. GM Liquid Products	20	3	2	0	0	0	×	0	0	0
8. GM Light Prods. 1	0	0	0	0	0	2	0	×	0	0
9 GM Light Prods. 2	0	0	0	0	0	4	0	0	×	0
10. GM Light Prods. 3	0	0	0	0	0	2	0	0	0	×

Table 5.3   Density Table of Multidivisional Firm

	Sums				Area				Density			
CEO & VP-HR	0	0	0	0	2	6	4	6	00	00	00	00
Fin/Tiny/Liq	22	0	0	0	6	6	6	9	3.66	00	00	00
Heavy & Light	38	10	0	0	4	6	2	6	9.50	1.66	00	00
Light, 1, 2, 3	0	0	8	0	6	8	6	6	00	00	1.33	00

Finally, even more simplification is attained by making a blockmodel from the density table, as in Table 5.4. The total number of approval requests (78) is divided by the total area of the matrix (n squared –n or 90) to get an average density for the entire table. Regions that fall below the average density are called zero blocks, those above, one blocks.

From this blockmodel, we surmise that Block 1 (CEO and VP of Human Resources) exercises direct control over all other officers except those belonging to Block 4 (General Managers of Light Operations 1, 2, and 3). Block 4 is subordinate to Block 3 (Heavy and Light Products), which in turn makes approval requests to the first two blocks. This shows us that even in terms of formal authority relationships (approval requests) the actual structure of relationships at the top of this organization is substantially different from that depicted in the organization chart. Using lines and arrows in the style of traditional charts, the real formal organization looks more like Figure 5.2.

If other kinds of relationships are considered, such as frequency of contact or dependence, still other patterns are found. Far from being an aberration, this example is typical of most organizations.

Table 5.4   Blockmodel of Multidivisional Firm

1. CEO and VP Human Resources	0	0	0	0
2. VP Finance, GM Tiny, GM Liquids	1	0	0	0
3. VP Heavy Prod., VP Light Prod.	1	1	0	0
4. GMs of Light 1, 2, 3	0	0	1	0

Figure 5.2   Multidivisional Network

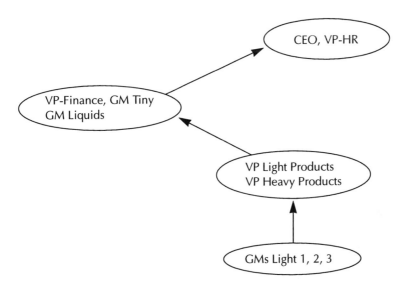

There is little need to construct a blockmodel out of adjacency matrices as small as this one. Visual inspection of the matrix will usually tell you all you need to know. However, in working with more than fifteen or twenty employees, blockmodels may be needed to identify broad social groupings and task units in the firm. Blockmodels are also good for comparing different organizations. By simplifying the complex web of contacts that make organizations work, blockmodels offer a simple but powerful shorthand of the real, working organization.

Advantages of Network Analysis

By now many of the advantages of network analysis should be obvious. Unlike the traditional approaches, network analysis is well suited to capturing both the formal and informal organizations and revealing important relationships between them. Not only do adjacency matrices indicate where relationships exist, they indicate the intensity or frequency of the relationships. An organization chart will not tell us which of a company's vice presidents have close ties to the CEO, or which managers maintain the greatest number and intensity of dependency relationships. Network analysis will.

Although adjacency matrices can be permuted according to hierarchical criteria, they don't have to be. Indeed, the great variety of interesting permutations that one adjacency matrix can yield is one indication of the diagnostic potential of network analysis. The same adjacency matrix can be permuted by department, indicating both internal cohesion and cross unit contacts; by specialization or function, indicating the comparative status and degree of integration of different functions; by physical location, reflecting the influence of facility design and allocation on the social fabric of the organization; or by seniority, ethnicity, age, workflow, merger status, and a host of other criteria.

For organizations trying to get beyond the traditional legacy of hierarchy and formal departmental boundaries, the breadth and flexibility of adjacency matrices suggest a much less deterministic way of conceptualizing organization structure, one much less tied to formal chain of command. Moreover, network analysis uses the actual perceptions of the people involved in the structure rather than uncritically imposing formal-mandated relationships handed down from top management in an organization chart. This makes it inherently more participative in nature.

Network analysis simultaneously expresses micro and macro aspects of the organization. One can look at the organization as a whole by computing a blockmodel based on a departmental or divisional permutation of the adjacency matrix. Equally easily, it is possible to print out the vectors of individual employees or the submatrices of small work groups in order to observe interactions at the shop floor or office levels. This attribute of network analysis also makes it easier to deal with the "lumpyness" that Mintzberg (1979) and others have observed in organizations.

Finally, for those working in small organizations, the richness of detail provided by network analysis, coupled with the comparatively small numbers involved, means that it is possible to paint a truly exhaustive portrait of the internal workings of the organization simply by handing out and retrieving a few sheets of paper and entering the resulting data. In the next chapter I provide detailed examples of how this can be done and of the results interpreted using real world cases.

6

Network Analysis in Action:
The Eastern Title Company
and Gottlich Hospital

This first case is particularly interesting because it illustrates how social networks interact with other elements of the activity system. It is also referred to heavily in Chapter 7, on cause maps. Because the case is used so extensively to illustrate important ideas and techniques, we need to describe both the title business and this particular company in some detail. As in all cases in this book, names and inconsequential details have been altered to protect the identity of the company. (Some of this material can be found in Nelson and Mathews 1991a.)

Eastern Title is a land title company operating in a community of around five hundred thousand located on the Southern Seaboard. The firm has been in existence for almost twelve years, experiencing rapid growth from six original employees to its present total of over eighty. The company is privately held and guards its financial figures jealously, but reliable sources indicate that Eastern Title is doing very well. The original founders have grown wealthy even while financing ET's growth out of operating revenues. Market share is around 40 percent, considerably above the nearest competitor, which holds around 13 percent of the market.

The community is growing rapidly, and ET plans to pick up an increasing share of business generated by new construction through continued emphasis on customer service and professionalism. A persistent problem, however, has been the ongoing search for an organization structure that will permit growth while maintaining the technical integrity and service orientation of the firm.

The Title Business

The purpose of a title company is to officially record real estate transactions and insure those transactions against legal errors and fraud on the part of buyer or seller. The local title company represents national underwriters in much the same way that an independent insurance agent may sell insurance from different companies. There is, however, a fundamental difference between an insurance broker and a title company. If one of the parties to a transaction suffers losses because of error on the part of the title company, the title company itself, rather than the national underwriter, may have to pay damages. Frequent losses covered by the underwriter can result in suspension of representation or even suspension of the state license required to record transactions.

Other, smaller losses which do not fall into the underwriter's categories are also covered by the title company and may run over $100,000 per year for a medium-sized firm. As a result, care and accuracy are of utmost importance in title work. Seemingly trivial errors can cause major losses. This need for care and precision is compounded by the complexity of the title examination and closing process.

A great number of documents must be gathered and evaluated in order to transfer ownership of real estate. The precise legal meaning and legal validity of each document and its relation to the present transaction must be verified before insurance can be issued or property rights transmitted. To do this accurately requires years of practice. Even title people with a decade or more of experience often need to call upon more knowledgeable experts for help with difficult questions. Those with five years or less experience cannot function adequately without access to a more experienced resource person.

The training of a title official (there are two general types, examiners and closers) is accomplished through a long informal apprenticeship. The intricacies of the title process are not taught in law schools or real estate courses, nor are they codified in any unitary body of literature. Some general principles exist, but the application of these principles takes frequent unexpected turns even for the initiated. Even the simplest of documents can contain surprises or exceptions invisible to all but the most expert. This endemic scarcity of expertise poses unique organizational and human resource problems.

Workflow at Eastern Title

Eastern Title has developed one of the most sophisticated and highly automated examination systems in the business. The title process begins when a client (usually a realtor) contacts the company with a request for a title search to verify the legal disposition of a given property. A title search is usually requested because the property in question is for sale or is about to be sold. An order form is filled out providing the names of the inquirer and the owners of the property, a legal description, and other data. Not infrequently, part of this information is not available or is incorrect, disrupting subsequent steps in the work process.

Order information is entered into a computer file, where it is stored until the transaction is finished and all funds disbursed. In addition to the information mentioned, the individual in charge of the job and the whereabouts of the job in the workflow are included and are updated periodically.

Chain and Search

Once the title search has been officially opened, the examination process may begin. Clerks in Chain-and-Search locate all documents pertinent to the property in question and record these in proper order for subsequent analysis by skilled examiners. Most of these documents are listed in one of two computer files, the geo and alpha files. The geo file contains a list of documents relevant to the physical property. The alpha file lists documents relevant to the individuals and to claims that may exist against their real estate holdings. Records of divorces, bankruptcies, and liability lawsuits are typical of documents indexed in this file. Once the pertinent documents have been identified through computer search, microfilms of documents are secured from the company's archives and copies are made. Maintenance of complete, accurate, and accessible records of legal transactions in the title company's jurisdiction is one of the firm's most important activities, and several full-time employees are retained expressly for this purpose.

Examination

Chain-and-search delivers a file containing the above-described documents to one of several examiners who will evaluate the legality of previous transmissions of the property in question and the validity of any claims against the property or its owners. Reasonable proficiency as an examiner can be acquired in about three years, but real expertise takes ten years or more to develop. For this reason, there is frequent consultation among examiners about technical questions. The greater one's experience, the more frequently one is consulted. The head of the examination department at Eastern Title spends about 70 percent of his time responding to the questions of the five examiners and other employees of the firm.

Upon completing analysis, the examiner notes any questions or irregularities on the file folder containing all documents. The file is then sent to the party who ordered the search, or to the policy department if insurance is to be written.

Policy

The policy department is responsible for determining the insurability of the proposed transaction and for writing the actual policy instrument to be used.

The policy department also records the final transaction with the county. This process contains three phases. First, the head of the policy department reviews the observations of the examiner and determines what, if any, exigencies must be met before title insurance can be issued. This requires thorough understanding of the logic of title examination plus a detailed knowledge of the requirements of the various underwriters represented by the company. The department head notes any requirements on the file, which then goes to a less experienced employee who reexamines the file and issues a commitment, an agreement to insure a title if stipulated requirements are met.

The greater the experience of the commitment writer, the less attention the department head must give to the file. Routine transactions receive only a cursory review before going to an experienced commitment writer; more complex cases require more involvement by the head of policy. All commitments are reexamined by the head of policy before being sent to clients.

After the client has satisfied the terms of the commitment and the transaction has taken place, the actual policy is issued. The policy writer holds a position separate from the commitment writer and reviews the transaction again before issuing a policy. Once the policy is issued, the final transaction is officially recorded at the county courthouse by a clerk who performs yet another check and hand carries transaction documents to the courthouse for microfilming.

After being recorded, the file containing all information on the transaction is "ditched." Documents from the transaction are put in a stipulated order and microfilmed, then filed in a warehouse. The computer file which accompanies the transaction is also placed on inactive status.

Closing

All of the functions described to this point come together when the closer meets with buyer and seller to witness the transaction, obtain necessary signatures, receive and disburse monies, and tie up any unfinished details relating to the transfer of the property.

Although the examination and policy departments compile and analyze the documents necessary for a transaction, final responsibility rests with the closer. The closer reevaluates the entire file and reaches a decision about the willingness of the company to officially sanction and record the deal (and assume the risk for any errors made). This means that the technical ability of the closer should equal or surpass that of the examiner.

In addition, the closer issues a financial statement of all of the charges generated by the transaction, identifying who is responsible for each amount. This requires a detailed knowledge of financial legalities and conventions beyond those required by the examination process.

The most challenging task of the closer, however, is to mediate between two parties whose interests are inherently at variance, in addition to third parties such as realtors and lending institutions. This must be done while protecting the interests of the title company by avoiding losses due to inaccuracy or fraud.

Dilemmas Faced by Closers. Business comes to the company through the closer. A popular closer attracts a large following of real estate agents and others who refer work to the firm. Parties frequently request that a specific closer take care of their title transfer. For this reason, closers spend considerable effort courting customer loyalty and attempting to resolve disputes between clients in an amicable manner. Every effort is made to accommodate the desires of repeat customers, often putting pressure on the production departments (examination and policy) for rush work.

The position of closers at the boundary of the organization makes them the focus of conflicting forces—fast service to customers may compromise the integrity of the examination process, while slow service may lose clients. (The state fixes fees for title work, so service rather than price is the object of competition between firms.) Untempered zeal in adhering to legalities may upset customers, but irregularities can cost the company its state license or underwriter services. Favorable treatment of one party in a transaction may alienate the other party, but impartial treatment may leave both parties unsatisfied. Meticulous defense of the title company's interests may generate ill will, but laxity creates losses for the firm.

Because of the complexity of the job, its relative status, and the importance of individual personalities in gaining and retaining business, closers tend to have a very individualized approach to their jobs. Each closer has an assistant to help with paper work. The closer and his or her assistant form a close social unit which is not easily controlled through typical managerial techniques. Eastern Title has two closing departments, one dealing primarily with residential transactions, the other with the transmittal of commercial property.

The work done in each department is similar, but commercial closings are fewer in number, higher in value, and more complex from a technical standpoint. With four closers and nine support personnel, the commercial department closes about the same dollar volume of business as the residential department with six closers and nine support staff. The president and two senior vice presidents of the firm are attached to the commercial department, and in addition to their executive activities they still close commercial business.

Support Departments

Two purely support components exist in addition to the production and closing areas. Data processing develops, implements, and maintains supporting information systems. Because of the uniqueness of the title business, software for storing and manipulating title information is developed in-house. Standard bookkeeping and payroll packages are also maintained. Eastern Title is a pioneer in the use of computers in the title business and is still developing and implementing innovative software to further automate the examination, policy, and closing process. A large backlog of projects will keep the two full-time programmers busy for a long time to come.

In addition to developing and maintaining computing capacity, data processing also collects and enters the legal information on properties and individuals that serves as the basis for subsequent production processes. The proper coding of these data is an art in and of itself, requiring understanding of complex legal conventions and their translation into a standardized coding process, and accuracy is of the essence. Legal transactions and litigations must be entered daily, so both speed and quality are necessary.

Personnel able to work quickly and accurately on such a complex task are rare indeed, especially considering the relatively low status associated with data entry. In an attempt to deal with this problem, more experienced coders spend most of their time checking the work of newer employees.

Data processing also carries out "ditching," mentioned earlier, by microfilming files and performing one last verification of names and legal descriptions of property before officially closing the file and sending it to archives.

Accounting

The accounting department fulfills traditional bookkeeping functions in addition to tasks unique to the title business. Closing statements generated by commercial and residential departments must be reconciled and fees entered in the firm's books. Monies taken in escrow are sometimes invested for the short term. Commissions of real estate agents, legal fees, and other disbursements arising from the closing are handled by bookkeeping. Losses and their sources are also catalogued and analyzed by bookkeeping. The role of the title company as an intermediary for transactions involving large sums makes the tasks of this unit more complex than would be the case in other firms of this size.

Accounting works closely with closing in dealing with transaction related financial matters. The identification of bookkeeping mistakes causing losses to the company is sometimes a bone of contention between accounting and closing, because both departments are responsible for calculations that must square one with the other.

Other Personnel

In addition to these departments, a small marketing department (three people) is charged with promoting the company, and a group of couriers or runners hand-carry documents between financial institutions, the court-house, clients, and offices of the title company. A separate branch, employ-ing six people, takes care of closings in a distant sector of town, but relies on the central offices for all title searches and support services. These units are not considered in the analyses of this chapter, but they will be included in a later chapter.

Evolution and Management Structure

The current president and two executive vice presidents founded Eastern Title eleven years ago after an unsuccessful bid to buy the title company at which they were employed. Several employees came with them to the new company, creating a strong, cohesive nucleus from which the firm evolved. A strong emphasis on service coupled with solid technical knowledge brought rapid growth, making ET the largest title company in the community.

Like many young companies founded by a dynamic entrepreneur, ET was initially managed almost singlehandedly by the CEO, with the assis-tance of the two other founders. No major decision and few minor ones were made without active consultation and approval of the president. As the need for separate departments arose, working supervisors were chosen to head the examination, policy, residential, closing, and support areas.

The use of working managers was partly due to the small size of the firm and to the philosophy of the founder that managers need to stay close to the operation of the business, but more fundamentally because of the im-portance of human capital to the title business. Due to the need for exten-sive consultation with more experienced employees, ET's most knowledge-able and capable people could not be severed completely from day-to-day operations. The tendency for clients to prefer specific closers and the status associated with closing exacerbated this need.

This arrangement, which worked well initially, began to overload execu-tive management, slow information flow, and stymie decisionmaking as the firm grew. In an attempt to ease the situation, department heads were formed into standing committees that addressed general areas of concern such as production, closing, marketing, and company policy.

The new committees facilitated coordination between areas and were helpful in generating novel ideas and suggestions, but executive manage-ment continued to be overburdened with operational details. As the firm grew to more than seventy employees, a consensus began to emerge among both key employees and the founders that a more fundamental change was needed, probably in the form of a middle management layer of some sort.

After a meeting with key staff, the founders established what it called a corporate management team composed of the department managers of examination, policy, data processing, accounting, residential and commercial closing departments. This group was charged with full operational management responsibility, with the understanding that "executive management (i.e., the founders) would attend the first team meetings and give direction from time to time." The previous committees continued, subject to any alteration that the new management team might stipulate. The formal structure, then, looked like Figure 6.1.

This step had several repercussions, none of them initially positive. Team meetings took a large amount of the time of department heads. This generated complaints from subordinates who frequently required consultation with their more experienced bosses. The team had difficulty reaching consensus on proposals, slowing the decision-making process. Moreover, decisions, once made, still required confirmation by top management. Not infrequently, decisions made by the corporate management team were vetoed by executive management.

Decisions enacted without top management approval were sometimes altered by executive management. This led to confusion among subordinates about who was authorized to make what decisions. The corporate management team was given the official mandate to make "decisions and policies that (were) mandatory and binding on all employees," but in practice no clear understanding of what the team could and could not do existed.

Now What?

About six months after the formation of the corporate management team, I was retained to assess the current structure and functioning of the organization. Not only were there questions about the overall management structure, there was concern about a number of operational questions, including frequent requests for rush jobs between closing, examination, and Policy; provision of incorrect information on titles, and financial errors incident to closings and final disbursement of funds. The complexity of the workflow and doubts about the management structure led me to to perform a network analysis of all eighty-two of the organization's employees. Below you will find density tables and blockmodels using a number of permutations (rearrangements) of the data.

The Frequency Matrix

Because of concern about information flow and collaboration between departments, I first divided up the data by department. A most striking result was immediately apparent in the diagonal cells of the frequency matrix, as shown in Table 6.1.

Figure 6.1   Eastern Title Organization Chart

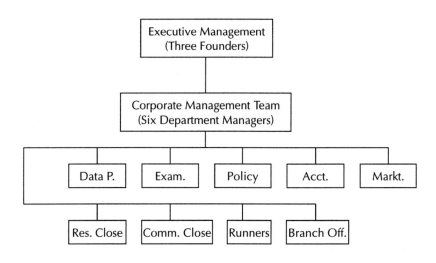

Table 6.1   Density Table of Frequency of Contact at Eastern Title

	Data P.	Exam.	Policy	Acct.	Resid.	Commer.
DP	10.23	3.19	3.79	1.67	2.71	2.21
EX	3.64	24.8	6.66	1.55	4.03	3.61
PL	1.94	2.8	13.25	1.37	1.98	2.06
AC	1.84	1.25	2.45	51.79	6.61	7.23
RS	2.36	4.51	3.91	8.88	24.16	5.98
CM	2.58	4.93	4.83	10.07	9.67	24.58

Blockmodel
(Cutpoint = 6.36)

DP	1	0	0	0	0	0
EX	0	1	1	0	0	0
PL	0	0	1	0	0	0
AC	0	0	0	1	1	1
RS	0	0	0	1	1	0
CM	0	0	0	1	1	1

Table 6.2 Partial Adjacency Matrix from Eastern Title (Exam, Policy, and Accounting Departments)

```
 0 10  5  1 10  3  5  5  1  0 | 2  0  2  0  0 | 0  0  0  0  0  0  0  0
15  0 10 10  0  0 15 15 10  5 | 0  3  0  0  0 | 0  0  0  0  2  0  0  0
30 30  0 50 50 50 50 50 50 50 |15 10 10 10  0 | 0  5  0  0  0  0  0  0
50 50 50  0 50 50 50 60 50 50 |25 50 50 35  0 | 0 10 10 10 10 10 10 10
50 50 50 99  0 50 50 50 50 50 | 2  5  2  2  1 | 0  0  0  0  2  0  0  0
 2  2  4  3  4  0  3  4  4  3 | 1  1  1  1  1 | 1  2  1  1  3  2  1  1
 5  5  5  5  5  5  0  5  5  5 | 3  3  3  2  0 | 0  2  0  1  1  0  1  0
50 50 50 50 50 50 50  0 50 50 | 2 15  4  0  2 | 0  0  1  2  3  0  1  1
25 25 30 15 15 15 15 15  0 15 |15 15  0 15  0 | 0  0  0  0  0  0  0  0
 5  5  5  5  5  5  5  5  5  0 | 5  5  5  5  5 | 0  4  2  4  3  1  3  3
 4  4  4  5  4  5  4  5  4  3 | 0  5  5  3  5 | 5  4  3  4  3  1  2  2
 3  3  3  5  3  3  5  5 15  0 |40  0 50 50 50 | 0  0  5  2  5  1  0  0
 1  1  1  1  1  0  1  2  4  1 | 5  5  0  5  5 | 0  0  0  0  0  0  0  0
 5  3  2  4  4  4  4  3  4  3 | 5  5  5  0  2 | 1  3  3  1  4  1  2  2
 0  0  0  0  0  0  0  1  3  0 | 5  5  5  5  0 | 0  1  0  0  0  0  0  0
 0  0  0  0  0  0  0  0  0  0 |20  0  0  0  0 | 0 99 99 99 99  3 99 99
 0  0  0  0  0  3  1  1  0  1 | 0  0  0  3  0 |99  0 20 25 25  5 99 99
 0  0  2  0  3  2  2  7  3  9 | 7  0  2  7  1 |99 99  0 99 99  4 99 99
 0  0  0  0  0  0  1  0  0  0 | 1  0  0  0  0 |10 10 10  0 10  1 10 10
 2  3  4  4  8  5  1 10  8  3 | 8 12  4  1  1 | 1 12 12 20  0  1 12  5
 1  1  1  1  1  1  1  1  1  1 | 1  2  1  1  0 | 2  2  2  3  1  0  2  2
 0  0  1  0  0  0  0  1  0  0 | 2  0  0  1  0 |99 99 99 99  0  2  0 99
 0  0  0  0  0  1  0  2  2  0 |20  0  3  0  0 |99 99 99 99 99  1 99  0
```

	Ex.	Pol.	Acct.
Exam	28.87	6.66	1.55
Policy	2.8	13.25	1.375
Accounting	1.25	2.4	51.79

Sums		
2238	333	124
140	265	55
100	98	2900

Area		
90	50	80
50	20	40
80	40	56

What Do You Mean, You Don't Understand?

If you don't see any "striking result," take heart. It takes more than one example to become comfortable with network analysis. This particular result, and sociomatrices generally, will be more easily understood if I recap the explanation of Chapter 5 using a portion of the adjacency matrix that yielded the densities found in Table 6.1.

What you see above is a 23 by 23 subset of the 82 by 82 matrix of weekly contacts from the title company. The twenty-three people are from the examination, (ten people), policy (five), and accounting (eight) departments. Remember that rows contain what people say about their contacts with others, while columns by definition record what others say about their contacts with a given individual.

Visual perusal of this part of the matrix reveals that examination and accounting entertain frequent interaction within their departments, while policy employees have much less internal contact. It would also appear that examination and policy share more frequent contact with one another than they do with accounting.

The density table allows for a more precise and compact comparison of cells and reduces the information therein to more manageable proportions. The number of contacts in a cell is divided by the area or number of possible relationships. Thus, the density of cell 3,1 (third row, first column) is 100/80 or 1.25. This can be interpreted as meaning that there is an average of 1.25 contacts per between the accounting and examination departments, if you listen to the accountants. If you ask the examination people (cell 1,3), there is an average of 1.55 contacts per week.

The density table confirms the impression that policy has a dearth of internal contacts, a sure indication of what I called low density in Chapter 2. One notes assymmetries also in off-diagonal cells. By asymmetry I mean group A claims more contact with group B that group B does with group A. The asymmetry between examination and accounting is small; 1.55 is close to 1.25. The asymmetry between examination and policy is large—6.66 versus 2.80. Assymmetries in dependence or approval matrices are easily interpreted as indicating the presence of hierarchy or a given workflow pattern. Assymmetries in the frequency matrix are not such a simple matter.

We tend to perceptually accentuate our contacts with important people (Ronnie Reagan? Sure we're friends. I talk to him all the time.) For this reason, assymmetries in frequency of contact are often indicative of status differences. Hence the fact that there is little disparity between the two numbers probably indicates that they view each other as peers. The assymmetries between examination (2.8) and policy (6.66), however, are probably an indication of policy's perception that examination is constantly making information requests.

With this short recapitulation lets go back up to the original frequency density table above and try to locate this most striking result on the diagonal, which is underlined for your convenience. Of course you see it now. Both data processing and examination have much lower internal contact than the other departments, while accounting has much higher internal density, causing us to wonder about dysfunctional high and low density in these departments.

Some judicious inquiries about these departments suggested that Policy was suffering some internal conflict and data processing experienced some friction and turnover, although not as seriously as examination. Accounting was generally perceived as rather isolated from the rest of the company. A strong professional identity and responsibilities quite different from those of the rest of the company seemed to have favored this insularity. I cannot say that the high internal density in accounting was actually dysfunctional, but I believe it did prejudice understanding of other units and limit the accountants' perspective.

The Dependency Matrix

In the light of these findings, it is interesting to compare the diagonals of the dependency matrix (see Table 6.3) to those of the frequency matrix. The degree to which people depend on each other to get their work done should provide a guide to how frequently they interact. One would expect that where interdependence is high and frequency of contact is low, performance difficulties would arise.

In comparing the two types of contacts, some mental adjustments must be made. Because we measure dependency on a scale of 1 to 6 rather than estimating the number of contacts per week, the dependency values are much lower and have less freedom to vary. Thus, small differences in dependency densities are of more relative importance than small differences in frequency densities.

After taking this difference into account we note that examination has relatively high internal dependence (2.7) and relatively low internal contact (13.25), while data processing has low dependence and frequency of contact (dependence: 1.37, frequency: 10.23). This may explain data processing's lesser woes.

This same approach of comparing dependence to frequency can be extended to relations between departments. Because there are so many possible relationships (thirty for each type of contact), it is best to work with the blockmodel, examining individual densities only when more detail is de-

Table 6.3 Density Table of Dependence at Eastern Title

	Data P.	Exam	Policy	Acct.	Resid.	Commer.
DP	1.37	0.52	0.37	0.28	0.23	0.24
EX	0.54	2.42	0.80	0.33	0.86	1.15
PL	0.32	1.16	2.70	0.60	0.77	0.94
AC	0.47	0.34	0.30	2.75	1.29	1.85
RS	0.40	1.11	1.11	1.38	1.74	0.85
CM	0.64	1.50	1.38	1.78	1.11	2.19

Blockmodel
(Cutpoint = 1.2)

DP	1	0	0	0	0	0
EX	0	1	0	0	0	1
PL	0	0	1	0	0	0
AC	0	0	0	1	1	1
RS	0	1	1	1	1	0
CM	0	1	1	1	0	1

sired. Remember that the blockmodel is a kind of shorthand of the density table in which cells above the mean are represented by a one, below the mean by a zero.

As we look at the frequency blockmodel (I repeat the frequency and dependency blockmodels as Table 6.4, for the sake of convenience), we see in the lower righthand corner a clump of one blocks connecting accounting, residential and commercial to each other but not to data processing, examination, or policy.

Introducing Propinquity

This is suspicious because we know that examination and policy provide important inputs for the closing process. We also know that there are problems with inaccuracies and rush jobs between closing, examination, and policy. Our suspicions are confirmed when we look at the Dependence matrix and find both closing departments dependent on examination and policy. The closing and accounting units appear to form a giant clique that is isolated from the prior components of the activity system despite their dependence on them.

What may have caused this strange scenario? No doubt the common perspective and similar activities of the closing functions are partly to

Table 6.4   Frequency versus Dependence Blockmodels

Frequency Blockmodel (Cutpoint = 6.36)						Dependence Blockmodel (Cutpoint = 1.2)					
DP	1	0	0	0	0	0	1	0	0	0	0	0
EX	0	1	1	0	0	0	0	1	0	0	0	1
PL	0	0	1	0	0	0	0	0	1	0	0	0
AC	0	0	0	1	1	1	0	0	0	1	1	1
RS	0	0	0	1	1	0	0	1	1	1	1	0
CM	0	0	0	1	1	1	0	1	1	1	0	1

blame. This, however, does not explain their frequent contacts with inward-looking, insular accounting. As it turns out, data processing, examination, and policy are located on two different floors of a separate, rented building across the street. The large, centrally located body of closers in the original location has developed an intense social life to which the small group of accountants has been sucked in by virtue of their physical proximity (some academics say propinquity).

It may seem absurd that thirty yards and two flights of stairs would make such a difference, but if you are an experienced manager, and you think about it, I'm sure you will be able to recall similar situations in which accidents of physical layout have caused major wrinkles in the social and operational fabric of an organization.

Another Propinquity Story

In my professorial life, I have worked for or visited a variety of business schools. It is probably not coincidental that the most cantankerous and the most peaceful school had the most organized and the most haphazard facilities respectively. School A was constantly fighting, department against department, department against the dean's office—a real zoo. Interestingly enough, school A's departments were all self-contained, each with a door leading from the hall into a suite of offices with its own secretarial staff, office supplies, and duplicating facilities.

The departments had a separate floor, the administration had its own floor, and the basement contained a computer laboratory and some classrooms. The layout obviated the need for people from different sectors to interact with one another informally. And because formal interactions were usually about divisive things like budgets and dean candidates, a very competitive if not divisive atmosphere developed.

The building for school B was a rambling, random affair that juxtaposed classrooms with faculty offices, and due either to an administrator's oversight or foresight (probably the former), put accountants next to marketers and statisticians next to business communications instructors. Xerox facilities and faculty mailboxes were in front of the dean's office, and the departmental offices were next to each other. In sum—a real zoo.

As a result of the confusion, faculty of different disciplines were always bumping into each other, as well as students, administrators, and office personnel. Result: in the building laid out like a zoo, people behaved like human beings—lots of interaction, lots of interdisciplinary projects, lots of cooperation. In the "organized" building, the people spent enormous amounts of time biting, clawing, and hissing at others not of their species.

The moral of both stories: Physical layout has enormous social consequences and should be thought about seriously. If your layout is suboptimal you may be able to foster network connections to overcome some liabilities, or if your network structure is suboptimal, you may be able to move people around in a way that improves the network. In any event, think seriously about how you use space (see Davis [1984] and Oldham and Notchford [1983] for interesting articles about this).

The Approval Matrix

Examination of internal (diagonal) densities and comparison of frequency and dependence blockmodels shed light on some of the operational problems in the activity system. The approval matrix, which deals with formal administrative requests, is usually a good tool for analyzing how the official management structure of the firm behaves. My perusal of the approval data suggested two things (see Table 6.5).

First, the approval matrix is rather sparse. The mean density for the entire approval matrix is .32 for monthly approval requests versus 6.36 for weekly frequency of contact. This suggests that most of the interaction in this firm is informal rather than formal. Given recent accuracy problems, it may be time for this young but rapidly growing firm to institute a few more formal managerial controls so that things don't fall through the cracks. Residential closing, which processes the greatest number of transactions of the two departments, has a rather low internal approval density (.93). It is probably a prime candidate for more formal supervision. The intent here is not to generate frivolous complexity but to identify those procedural errors and inefficiencies that can be remedied by installing formal procedures that provide maximum benefit with minimum bureaucracy.

A second concern that arises upon examination of the approval matrix, more specifically the blockmodel, is the preponderance of approval requests made to closing, particularly commercial closing. This can be verified by counting the number of 1's in all columns and noting that Commercial re-

Table 6.5   Density Table of Approvals at Eastern Title

	Data P.	Exam	Policy	Acct.	Resid.	Commer.
DP	0.77	0.19	0.15	0.21	0.14	0.35
EX	0.02	0.51	0.00	0.23	0.00	0.07
PL	0.03	0.00	0.50	0.25	0.00	0.12
AC	0.75	0.01	0.10	2.33	0.36	1.21
RS	0.19	0.27	0.34	0.62	0.93	0.46
CM	0.03	0.16	0.23	0.66	0.25	2.30

Blockmodel
(Cutpoint = .319)

DP	1	0	0	0	0	1
EX	0	1	0	0	0	0
PL	0	0	1	0	0	0
AC	0	0	0	1	1	1
RS	0	0	1	1	1	1
CM	0	0	0	1	0	1

ceives three nondiagonal ties versus only one for all three departments located across the street. Reviewing the organization chart, I discovered that all three vice presidents are in commercial closing. This is understandable given the fact that the company was founded by three closers, but it is likely to cause considerable imbalance in the activity system. In order to secure needed coordination with examination and policy, some other administrative arrangement would be preferable.

The Hierarchical Permutation

Indeed, one objective behind the formation of the corporate management team (basically composed of all department heads) was to facilitate coordination by putting operational concerns under the authority of a balanced group. But the corporate management team was having difficulty. A partition (dividing up) of the network data by the new hierarchy, as in Table 6.6, suggests reasons why.

Of all categories—even nonsupervisors—the corporate management team had the least internal contact, suggesting that despite their long meetings, they were not collaborating frequently on operational concerns. Meanwhile, executive management had the highest frequency of internal contact. Compare corporate management team's 4.58 weekly contacts to executive's 15.8. Such frequent contact maintains group identity and team

Table 6.6 Densities of Hierarchical Grouping

Weekly Contact

	Exec	CMT	Sup.	Others
Executive Management	15.83	6.58	9.67	4.70
Corporate Man. Team	4.17	4.58	9.40	4.67
Supervisors	6.33	7.15	5.40	6.71
Other Employees	5.79	6.44	7.54	6.18

Dependence

	Exec	CMT	Sup.	Others
Executive Management	4.33	2.33	3.13	1.17
Corporate Man. Team	1.42	1.08	1.05	0.64
Supervisors	2.00	1.05	1.65	0.90
Other Employees	1.05	0.97	1.36	0.82

Approvals

	Exec	CMT	Sup.	Others
Executive Management	3.83	0.67	0.20	0.31
Corporate Man. Team	2.42	20.8	1.55	0.30
Supervisors	2.87	1.20	0.55	0.05
Other Employees	0.88	0.78	0.77	0.22

spirit which, in my experience, greatly enhance a body's power vis-à-vis less cohesive groups.

As important as the dearth of internal contacts is, the pattern of external contacts in terms of both frequency and formal approvals is of greater concern. Expressed in blockmodel terms, a hierarchy normally should look like Table 6.7.

The above stairstep pattern means that top managers are not bothered with the affairs of the workers or managers except via the vice presidents. This lets top management worry about the big picture without being overloaded by operational matters that can be delegated.

Looking at the approval density table, we can discern a blockmodel something like Table 6.8.

Obviously the formal hierarchy is not achieving its filtering role. If we study the actual densities, it is apparent that virtually all levels still make more approval requests to executive management than they do to the corporate management team. Moreover, outside of the executive diagonal,

Table 6.7   Theoretical Hierarchy Blockmodel

CEO	1	0	0	0
Vice Presidents	1	1	0	0
Managers	0	1	0	0
Workers	0	0	1	1

Table 6.8   Hierarchy Blockmodel at Eastern Title

Exec.	1	0	0	0
CMT	1	1	1	0
Supervisors	1	1	0	0
Other	1	1	1	0

frequency of contact is almost random, demonstrating that the formal hierarchy has almost no role in the ebb and flow of contacts throughout the firm. Taken together, these numbers indicate a firm that has grown in volume and people but retains the networks (and probably the culture) of a startup.

It is probably time for a little more bureaucracy, less fluid priorities, and a little more explicit social engineering. If I were running the outfit I would probably hire or promote an office manager with lots of clout to tighten the ship, disband the corporate management team and either search for quarters under one roof or, failing that, have policy and accounting change offices.

Lessons from the Case

Many if not most of the observations in this case are indicative of general principles that seem to apply across a variety of organizations I have known. To summarize my experience using the Eastern Title case as a backdrop, I offer the following guidelines for networks.

Internal Density

Beware of excessively high or excessively low (especially low) densities within units. Low density leads to conflict, insufficient coordination, and errors. High density leads to smugness and isolation from other units, and it may provoke interdepartmental conflict and errors. Only departments like auditing that require almost no coordination with the rest of the organization should be unconcerned about high density. As a rule, diagonal densities of departments should be much higher than off-diagonal densities; if ties between departments are stronger than within, the purpose of departmentation is defeated.

Frequency and Dependence

Frequency of contact and degree of dependence should be somewhat balanced. Low frequency of interaction accompanied by high levels of dependence are often indicative that interpersonal disputes are influencing the quality or volume of a unit's work. When this happens between work units, lack of formal coordination mechanisms are often at fault, especially in younger or rapidly growing organizations.

Approval Matrices

Comparison of the approval matrix with the frequency matrix provides a measure of the degree of formal management control in various departments and in the organization as a whole. The degree of formal control needed varies by task and organization, but excessively high approval-to-frequency ratios (over one approval for four contacts) or low ones (less than one in ten) indicate problems. Hierarchical relationships are found by examining assymmetries in the approval matrix. If actual approval requests are substantially different from the formal hierarchy, some kind of dysfunction probably exists. If densities of top managers with lower hierarchical levels are similar to those of proximate levels, insufficient delegation, bypassing, or poor design of the hierarchy are a problem.

The Gottlich Hospital Case

A very different but similarly instructive case is that of an 120-bed hospital owned by a monastic order of the Catholic church. Unlike our young title company, this is a very old organization, owned by a very old religious order. Also unlike the title company, which lacks historical and bureaucratic baggage, Gottlich has an excess.

During most of its history, the hospital had emphasized charitable service, with little emphasis on financial performance. With the passage of time and changes in the structure of the U.S. health care industry, the hospital began to suffer financial pressures, low morale, and strategic indecision. As a result of these deteriorating conditions, Gottlich Hospital (a pseudonym) hired its first lay hospital administrator in 1984. (Heretofore, the head of the order was also the head of the hospital.) The new administrator was formerly chief operating officer at a larger local hospital and brought with him several subordinates and professional associates. Thereafter he made several other hires. After about a year in office, conditions had not improved despite a rather thorough reorganization.

A CONCOR partition of the data showed a rather confused amalgam of persons and contacts that gave little impression of systematic structure or order. I hit paydirt though when, at the suggestion of the former corporate counsel for the institution, I divided the management staff into three groups—those who came from the CEO's former hospital, those who were hired after his arrival, and those who were already there when he arrived—as shown in Table 6.9.

This partitioning is akin to the social group approach to identifying organizational culture discussed in Chapter 3. We have identified social groups that we believe are significant in the history of the organization and have singled them out for study. The only difference is that we are looking at the networks of these groups rather than their culture.

The density tables above are so eloquent as to almost dispense with comment. The new CEO and his pals from the old hospital form a tightly knit group that has the last word on what goes on in the hospital. Just look at group 1's column for the approval matrix. The CEO's clique is strongly tied to a group of newcomers that has some internal identity but is more strongly tied to the CEO's clique than they are to one another (see the density table for frequency of contact). Check out group 2's internal versus external contacts. The new hires also have some formal power of their own, but are clearly subordinate to the CEO's clique.

The old timers are so disenfranchised and weak that they don't talk to much of anybody, and they have little internal cohesion. Their internal ties are about equal to their external densities, and are much lower than the other two groups (see frequency densities). They are formally subordinated to both CEO and new-hire groups. Note that the formal approval matrix displays the same bypassing pattern as Eastern Title, except that we are not dealing with a formal hierarchical permutation here.

This hospital went out of business the year after data were collected. I do not know to what degree the network configuration described above contributed to the closing, but I suspect it had a role. This hospital clearly had cultural problems, and I regret not having access to CVAT data to substantiate them. But my discussions with former employees revealed that the charitable orientation of the order and the commercial orientation of the new management never did quite mix.

My own speculation is that the new CEO's coup left the old timers so demoralized that it was not possible to implement his plans for modernization. Using my terms, I would say that the rapid introduction of some many new human elements into the activity system overwhelmed what was already there. I suspect also that the sudden influx of new people probably also caused considerable confusion about which boundary maintenance

Table 6.9 Permutation of Hospital by Hire

Frequency			
From CEO's Hospital	5.5	3.11	2.17
New Hires	3.58	2.87	2.08
Old Timers	1.79	1.33	1.25
Approvals			
From CEO's Hospital	1.87	0.5	0.08
New Hires	2.36	1.0	0.41
Old Timers	2.21	1.42	1.42

mechanisms should remain intact and which should come down. If I had had my way in this case I probably would have brought fewer people in from outside and would have placed new hires physically and hierarchically close to old timers. But of course hindsight is 20/20, and the new CEO probably felt the need for decisive measures.

A Little More Theory

The cases and mechanics we have been through so far have hopefully given you a feel for what to do when you get your hands on some sociomatrices. Although it takes looking at fifty firms or so to become really proficient at reading the tea leaves of network data, if you are working with data from your own company or agency, your lack of experience with the methodology will be largely offset by your personal knowledge of the social territory.

Even so, figuring out what your network should look like and how to bring it about is not a transparent matter. With CVAT data you at least have the ideal profile to look at and the intuitive meanings of the various dimensions. The network situation, on the other hand, is much more abstract and less intuitive. For this reason, it will be worthwhile to look at some more rudiments of theory for clues to improving networks.

Tie Strength: Weak, Strong, and Very Strong

Earlier we spoke of three types of relations that tend to be important in organizations: frequency of contact, dependence, and approvals. A number of other types of relations can be important, including kinship, club membership, or information exchange. However, one of the most important aspects of a tie is not the type of relationship but its strength. Harvard Professor

Mark Granovetter (1973) first stumbled across the phenomenon of tie strength in a study of job-seeking behavior.

He found the old adage "it's not what you know but who you know" to be true, but in a way different from what we would usually expect. Granovetter found a major difference between the pay levels and status of jobs that were located by formal means (i.e., answering want ads, sending résumés) and those obtained through personal contacts. So far, no surprises. What is surprising is the intensity or strength of relationship that netted the best jobs.

In talking to people about the contacts that they used in job searches, Granovetter found that some involved frequent contact, considerable warmth or affect, and a sense of reciprocity or mutual obligation. These he called strong ties. Others, which he called weak ties, involved low levels of all three—infrequent contact, little sense of mutual obligation, and neutral affect. Interestingly, the best jobs were found through weak ties rather than strong ties. Intuitively, we would expect the opposite, that people would locate the best jobs through the favors of close friends.

Why the Old-Boy Network Didn't Work

Granovetter's explanation for this apparent contradiction is ingenious. He argued that our strongest friendships tend to be interconnected in such a way as to restrict access to information from outside our particular clique. In other words, my best friends are friends with each other, forming a self-limiting little circle that is not likely to pick up information from far afield. Weak ties, on the other hand, are likely to reach people distant from ourselves in both social and geographic terms, thus increasing the likelihood that a weak tie will bring us valuable information from afar.

Later studies by Granovetter and others have identified further consequences of tie strength. The tendency for us to become close to people much like ourselves makes strongly tied groups harmonious and highly cohesive but resistant to change and intolerant of diversity—one more manifestation of the harmony–flexibility dilemma we encountered in our study of culture. When strongly tied groups occur in organizations, they can cause polarization, factionalization, and conflict.

Weak ties, on the other hand, appear to be useful conduits for information and the spread of novel ideas, but their lack of reciprocity and warmth means that they have limited value for mobilizing concerted action. Studies of social networks under crisis conditions reveal that less conflict and better coordination is found in organizations that have strong ties cutting across units compared to organizations where strong ties are limited within units (Krackhardt and Stern, 1988).

Diffusing, Bridging, and Bonding

In my own work, I have identified three levels of tie strength—weak, strong, and very strong. Each appears to play a somewhat different role in organizations (Nelson and Mathews 1991a). Weak ties, as mentioned above, diffuse information and novelties. Strong ties—essentially friendly but not intimate professional contacts—coordinate and mobilize activity. Very strong ties are intimate friendships that extend well beyond work requirements. These provide support in times of adversity, help sort out and interpret life in the organization, and offer satisfying interactions that enable people to dedicate large amounts of time and emotional energy to the workplace.

To summarize their characteristics and keep the strength levels straight, I like to call them bonding, bridging, and diffusing ties. Very strong ties bond people together, strong ties provide bridges between them, and weak ties assure the diffusion of information.

Tie Strength in Organizations

I have found that all three strength levels have their place in organizations, but that their comparative distribution and location can be important, and the ease with which they are managed varies greatly. Ample weak ties are necessary to provide flexibility and responsiveness, but they do not always develop automatically. Occasional social events, formal sign-off requirements, and other mechanisms may need to be implemented to assure that they take place. However, with a little thought and effort, it is possible to stimulate an adequate level of weak ties.

In smaller organizations, strong ties tend to develop by themselves within departments; and in fact they can easily become the dominant type of tie in the organization, leading to inflexibility and impermeable boundaries. The tendency for firms to develop an old-boy network of congenial but not intimate ties is particularly strong when the firm has been around for awhile and has gone through one or two purges of dissidents (see Chapter 3 on purges). Somewhat larger organizations may develop such old-boy networks within departments without extending strong ties to other organizational units, provoking the above-mentioned conflicts.

Unlike weak ties, then, little needs to be done to develop strong ties. Like weeds, they usually spring up pretty much by themselves, especially in smaller organizations, organizations with strong cultures, and organizations with people of similar backgrounds. (They may be harder to come by in larger concerns.) Unlike weeds, though, you do want some, and you want to make sure they are found in the right places—namely, between members of different units. This is probably best done through occasional transfers between functions and very careful management of office assignments to assure that people from departments who need coordination are located close to each other. As in the title case above, one of the most compelling arguments for a new facility or remodeling is to manage social relations through judicious manipulation of physical space.

Strong-tie networks that are becoming too dense can also be avoided by keeping staffing levels lean and making sure that higher-performing employees are more copiously rewarded than their lower-performing associates. Higher staffing levels generate surplus time for sociability and broad network building, while leaner staff means both fewer people to interact with and less time for strong-tie building. Similarly, differential rewards stimulate competition and retard collegiality somewhat, leading to weaker ties or very small numbers of very strong ties. Of course, you must be careful not to get carried away, lest you lose good people to overwork and conflict.

Bonding or very strong ties can be highly motivating and enriching for some people, and I believe that high-performing organizations always feature bonding ties among several key players. Unfortunately, bonding ties tend to follow their own logic and are rather impervious to premeditated manipulation by managers. They depend little on staffing levels or reward systems and once in place, they can be very durable across time and space. At best, an organization can create a favorable environment for development of bonding ties.

Strong bonds are most common between people of similar values, abilities, and social backgrounds who have gone through hardships and stress together. The British regimental system, which recruits by geographic region and always moves as a unit, is an ideal environment for the formation of bonding ties. Sports teams often experience similar dynamics, and some companies attempt to replicate this atmosphere with varying degrees of success. Companies that are congenial to the development of mentoring relationships are also likely to develop very strong ties between some younger and older employees. However, I believe that to a large degree bonding is serendipitous, and few concrete tactics will influence the incidence of bonding ties in an organization.

To partially substantiate my claims about the nature and differential desirability of the different tie strengths, I offer the statistics in Table 6.10, taken from a study of fourteen high- and low-performing protestant churches (Nelson and Mathews, 1991b).

The high performers have fewer strong ties than the low performers (43% versus 65% of all ties, respectively), suggesting that the old-boy network may have gotten out of hand in the low-performing churches, driving out innovation and making boundaries impermeable to new members. The high performers of course have many more weak ties than the lower performers, almost double the percentage. The number of very strong ties is very close, only a whisker higher for the high performers.

Table 6.10   Tie Strength by Performance

Tie Strength	High	Low
Very Strong	642 (8.41%)	384 (8.02%)
Strong Ties	3,315 (43.5%)	3,105 (64.8%)
Weak Ties	3,673 (48.1%)	1,298 (27.1%)

Checking now on the argument that organizations need strong ties between groups to function, consider another slice of data from the church study, as shown in Table 6.11.

The word "Internal" in this table means that these ties are found within groups or cliques. The cliques were identified by the CONCOR computer program on the disk that comes with this book. Remember (from Chapter 4) that CONCOR places people together based on the similarity of their responses, be they responses about culture, networks, or what have you. As a rule—not invariably, but as a rule—people with similar networks belong to the same social groups, so running CONCOR on social network data will identify cliques or groups of friends in an organization.

The External in the table means ties that cross over between groups. In other words, if Larry, Harry, and Terry are one group and Lester, Fester, and Nestor are another, a friendship between Larry and Nestor equals an external tie. A friendship between Larry and Harry is an internal tie. The table shows us that the high performers have a higher ratio of external to internal ties than the low performers, a ratio of 5.64 for high performers versus 3.64 for low performers. This means that in the higher performing organizations there are more Larry–Lester friendships than in the low performers. This, by the way, does not hold for weak and very strong ties. Strong ties evidently build a bridge between social groups that cannot be built using weak ties, and for which very strong ties are ill adapted.

Final Observations

Like culture, an organization's social network is one of those things that are very important but not very visible. The techniques that we have examined will make your networks more visible by providing detailed maps of people's interrelations. Like any map, sociomatrices and blockmodels take some getting used to before you can use than to find your way around, but I believe the effort is well worthwhile.

Perhaps the most important benefit of studying an organization's sociomatrices is not the actual knowledge one will gain of existing networks (useful as that may be), but rather how it provokes new ways of looking at

Table 6.11   External Versus Internal Ties by Performance (Strong Ties Only)

	High	*Low*
Internal	522	669
External	2,793	2,436

organizations. I will never look at your organization in quite the same way again once I've seen its sociomatrix. I realize that some relationships I thought were unimportant are actually critical, while other relationships are superfluous. More often, I will note that a relationship does not occur where it should, or it is of the wrong type. I will also start to see how the strengths and weaknesses of your company are influenced by by its networks. All of these insights are well worth the modest effort and expense of periodically collecting and analyzing network data.

7

Cognitive Maps:
Seeing the Invisible Causes

In the last two chapters you learned how to stuff the firm's social world into little sociometric boxes. I am now going to teach you how to do the same for the firm's mental life. "Why would I want to do that?" you ask. Because using matrices to represent the forces at work in your organization disciplines your thinking, enables members of the organization to clearly communicate their understanding of complex phenomena, and permits a number of clever mathematical manipulations that help to uncover potential weaknesses and problems before they turn into fiascoes.

The specific technique is called cause mapping or cognitive mapping, and although developed by academics (see the major work by Axlerod 1976), it is really quite simple. If you survived the network analysis chapters, this will be a snap.

In academic terms a cause map is a "mathematical representation of perceived causal relationships among variables" (Nelson and Mathews, 1991a: 380). In normal English, a cause map can be defined as a system of notation for recording how one thing influences another. The basic mechanics of cause mapping are quite simple. Different experts' approaches differ slightly, but the steps I outline here are common to most.

Steps in Cause Mapping

List Making

First, you get a number of people who know a subject matter well to make a list of what they consider to be the most important aspects of the subject. Next, reduce the list to a manageable number of factors, typically between eight and twelve. This is done by including first the factors that everyone mentioned and eliminating those mentioned by only one person. If the number of factors is still too large, consider eliminating factors mentioned later rather than earlier in people's lists. If possible, it is also wise to consult your experts about those factors you are inclined to omit; they may have other ideas.

It is also necessary when choosing variables for a cause map to make sure that factors are clearly defined and that they do not duplicate one another. For instance, one expert may specify speed while the other says turnaround time. But upon probing you will find that the words mean the same thing. Conversely, similar or identical terms may actually mean different things. Satisfaction may refer to customer satisfaction or employee satisfaction. By organization one person may mean physical neatness while another may mean work scheduling. It is good to have your respondents comment on a final draft of the factors and their definitions before proceeding.

Identifying Relationships

After the variable list is created, the people selected to participate in the study are asked to identify what causal relationship, if any, exists among each pair of variables. A positive causal relationship is identified by a 1, a negative relationship by a –1, and 0 indicates no relationship. This is easier done than said. Let's say our experts have identified job satisfaction, productivity, absenteeism, and quality as important variables to be included in a cause map.

The respondent simply asks, "Does an increase in satisfaction lead to increased productivity, decreased productivity, or does it have no influence?" The appropriate response (1, –1, or 0) is entered in the second column of the first row of the cause map. Next the respondent asks, "Does an increase in satisfaction lead to an increase in absenteeism, a decrease in absenteeism, or does it have no influence?" The response is entered in the third column of the first row, and so on. Once all the impacts of satisfaction on the other variables in the table have been identified, the first row is finished.

The next row begins in like manner: "Does an increase in productivity increase, decrease, or have no impact on satisfaction?" The response goes into the first column of the second row. "Does productivity increase, decrease, or not affect absenteeism?" The response goes into the third column of the second row. Note that we leave the diagonal blank or zero (i.e., the first column of the first row, the second column of the second row, and so on). Once we have posed and answered questions for all rows, we will have a square matrix with zeroes on the diagonal. A row will represent the influence of one variable on all other variables, and the corresponding column represents the influence of all other variables on that variable. The result will look something like Table 7.1.

In this cause map, the –1 in cell 1,3 (row 1, column 3) indicates that satisfaction reduces absenteeism, and the 0 in cell 3,1 indicates that absenteeism does not directly influence satisfaction.

Table 7.1   Example of Cause Map

	1	2	3	4
1. Satisfaction	0	0	−1	1
2. Productivity	1	0	0	0
3. Absenteeism	0	−1	0	−1
4. Quality	0	0	0	0

A More Complex Example: Back to Eastern Title

To illustrate why it is worth the trouble of translating straightforward statements of cause and effect into a funny box of ones and zeros will take a little more complex map that the one above. To economically supply such a map I will return to the Eastern Title case already familiar from the preceding chapter. In my interviews with the ET employees I was able to identify the variables perceived to be most important in the title business and how they interrelate. (You may need to reread the description of the title business from Chapter 6 to be more at ease with this cause map.) Below is a list of variables and their definitions:

Critical Variables in the Title Business.   1. Volume of Transactions. This can be defined operationally as the number of closings executed in a given time period. Because rates are fixed by the state, volume of transactions is closely linked to financial performance.

2. Speed of Work. The amount of time taken to process a title search, write a policy agreement, assemble, evaluate, and prepare closing documents—Speed of service is a major concern of clients.

3. Accuracy of Work. The number of legal, financial, or other errors made in recording and transmitting transactions, whether these errors result in losses or not.

4. Customer Satisfaction.

5. Losses. Monies paid to third parties to rectify or compensate errors in the title search, policy, or closing process.

6. Availability of Technical Expertise. The amount of time it takes to locate and obtain an unambiguous response to a technical question. This variable impacts on both speed and accuracy.

7. Ability to Resolve Clients' Concerns and Disputes. The interpersonal, communications, and technical capacity to respond adequately to client discontent, while simultaneously defending the legitimate interests of the title company and of other clients.

8. Ability to Prioritize Title Searches. The capacity to estimate the probable time a search will take, weigh the relative commercial importance of a

given search, and schedule searches in a manner that will optimize volume of transactions.

9. Morale. Employee morale.

10. Contacts with Clients or Prospective Clients. The title business is quite personalistic. Hence employee contact with real estate professionals is important in generating and maintaining business.

The professional judgment of members of Eastern Title regarding the interrelations between the variables above yields the cause map shown in Table 7.2.

Useful Numbers

Some very basic mathematical manipulations of the cause map can tell us several things about the title business that we would not otherwise know. By summing absolute values (that is, the number of 1's, independent of whether they are negative or positive) across rows, we learn how many other variables a specific variable affects directly. This sum is called an outdegree. The outdegrees for all ten variables are found in the far right column of the cause map. The outdegree for variable 6, Availability of Technical Expertise, is 7, indicating that expertise affects seven other variables.

Summing 1's by columns (again, independent of sign), we obtain the indegree, which indicates how many variables influence a given variable. Indegrees are located in the last row of the cause map. By subtracting indegrees from outdegrees, we find out which variables have the most general influence net of their susceptibility to other causal factors. For the Eastern Title map, indegree minus outdegree is depicted in Table 7.3.

The difference, which I call the net influence index, is useful in finding which variables can have the greatest impact on organizational performance with the least amount of headache. The net influence index suggests that the availability of technical expertise (variable 6) is an ideal lever for change, influencing seven other variables while being influenced by only one variable. That is, to change variable 6 in this business, few other factors in the organization must be dealt with, yet an improvement in variable 6 will improve a majority of the critical causal variables found in this organization. These summary statistics can be very useful in deciding where and when to take action when changes are needed. Even more interesting, though, is to identify those variables that influence each other—loops in cyberspeak.

Loops

Loops are found where variable A influences variable B, which influences variable A right back. Loops are all around us, and because of their spiraling

Table 7.2 Eastern Title Cause Map

1. Volume	0	−1	−1	0	1	−1	0	1	0	−1	9
2. Speed	1	0	−1	1	1	0	0	0	1	0	5
3. Accuracy	1	−1	0	1	−1	0	0	0	1	0	5
4. C. Sat.	1	0	0	0	0	0	0	0	1	0	2
5. Losses	0	0	0	1	0	0	0	0	−1	0	2
6. Expertise	1	1	1	1	−1	0	0	1	1	0	7
7. Resolve	1	0	0	1	−1	0	0	0	1	0	4
8. Prioritize	1	1	1	1	−1	0	0	0	1	0	6
9. Morale	1	0	1	1	−1	0	1	0	0	0	5
10. Contacts	1	0	0	1	0	0	1	0	0	0	3
Sums (Absolute Values)	8	4	5	8	7	1	2	2	7	1	45

Table 7.3 Eastern Title Net Influence Index

Variables	1	2	3	4	5	6	7	8	9	10
Outdegree	6	5	5	2	2	7	4	6	5	3
Indegree	−(8	4	3	8	7	1	2	2	7	1)
Net Influence Index	−2	1	0	−6	−5	6	2	4	−2	2

properties they can cause tremendous harm or good. Most of the loops we recognize easily are called deviation-amplifying loops. A deviation-amplifying loop exists when an increase in one variable leads to an increase in another or a decrease in one variable leads to a decrease in another. They are easily recognized because of their frequently spectacular results.

Some Dysfunctional Deviation-Amplifying Loops

Roger has problems on the job so he drinks to forget them, which erodes Roger's job performance, which leads to more problems on the job that provoke more drinking, which provokes more job problems, and so on. This is a classical deviation-amplifying loop. Here is another: Mary doesn't have enough money to pay cash so she charges purchases. Mary must pay interest on the purchases she charges. This means that Mary has less money so she charges a greater proportion of her purchases. Mary must therefore pay more interest so she charges more purchases, and so on. The buses run infrequently so fewer people ride the bus, so the city dispatches fewer buses, which means they run less frequently still, so fewer people ride the bus, and so on.

Some Desirable Deviation Amplifying Loops

I think that most of us are best at noticing dysfunctional loops, but there are also desirable deviation-amplifying loops. Fred exercises, which slows his metabolism and takes off weight. Because he is lighter, it is easier for Fred to exercise, so he exercises more. Because Fred exercises more, his metabolism slows more, and he takes off more weight. . . . Not only can deviation-amplifying loops provide desirable outcomes, they underlie most competitive advantages that firms develop. Frito-Lay sells a lot of product so it makes more frequent deliveries than its competitors. More frequent deliveries mean that its product is fresher, so Frito-Lay sells more product than its competitors. Wal-Mart sells cheaper than its competitors so it sells more. Because it sells more, it buys in greater quantity. Because it buys in greater quantity, it gets better discounts, allowing Wal-Mart to sell cheaper, and around it goes.

Deviation Limiting Loops

Not all loops are deviation amplifying; some tend toward balance over time. Although they do not produce as spectacular results, they can also be important. Thermostats are the archetypical deviation-limiting loops. The hotter it is, the more the metal in the thermostat curves until it trips the mechanism disconnecting the furnace. This causes the thermostat to cool, which flattens the metal until it trips the mechanism that starts the furnace.

Deviation-limiting loops are, of course, not confined to mechanical devices: The more patients a doctor has, the less time he or she has to spend with them, so she loses patients to doctors who have fewer patients. As she loses patients, she has more time to spend with them, which attracts more patients. The fact that one variable goes down while the other goes up tends toward equilibrium, hence the term deviation-limiting. As this example illustrates, one of the key things to remember when dealing with deviation-limiting loops is the need to balance trade-offs. Rather than suffering through all the disruptions of losing then gaining patients, our doctor friend would do well to find the exact balance point at which too many patients prejudice service and adjust his or her case load not to exceed that limit.

Explosive Clusters

It is very important for managers to know about the loops in their businesses. Disregarding deviation-limiting loops causes the organization to cycle erratically because trade-offs are not carefully managed; and it can also mean vicious circles that get out of hand or the loss of important competitive advantages. Even more dangerous are situations where more than one deviation loop intersect. For instance, poverty provokes overcrowding of living spaces. Overcrowding provokes disease. Disease, in turn, provokes poverty. Poverty also provokes drug use, which provokes further poverty. Drug use also provokes disease. Poverty provokes further overcrowding. The cause map might look something like Table 7.4.

This cause map is highly dense: out of a possible 12 connections there are 7. Such high density heightens the likelihood that several loops will intersect.

Several loops interacting can produce what Mausch (1985) calls an explosive cluster, that is, a situation in which intersecting loops consume all available resources and ultimately destroy the system. We see explosive clusters in both human and technical settings. When alcoholics finally hit bottom, it is because the various intersecting loops in their lives—alcohol tolerance, social adjustment, financial woes, work performance, and physical symptoms—have amplified each other to produce an explosive cluster. When nuclear reactors melt down, it is due to a similar intersection of cooling system defects damaging emergency backups which override normal control systems which prevents shutdown, leading to damaged containment systems, and so on.

Using Cause Maps to Find Loops and Clusters

A major, if not THE major, benefit of cause maps is their capability to quickly and clearly locate deviation-amplifying and -limiting loops as well as potential explosive clusters. This capability can help managers avoid problems that they might not even notice until it is too late. To see how this is done, let's look again at the poverty, overcrowding, disease, and drugs map suggested in Table 7.4.

We can identify loops here by looking at the row/column combination for a given variable (the i,j cell, as statisticians would say), then looking at the column/row combination (the j,i cell). A nonzero entry in both cells is indicative of a loop. If both entries have the same sign (positive or nega-

Table 7.4   Map with Explosive Cluster

	1	2	3	4
1. Poverty	0	1	1	1
2. Overcrowding	0	0	1	0
3. Disease	1	0	0	0
4. Drug Abuse	1	0	1	0

tive), we have a deviation-amplifying loop. If the signs are different, we have a deviation-limiting loop.

For instance, in row 1, column 2, we see that poverty favors overcrowding. In row 2, column 1, however, there is a zero, meaning overcrowding does not cause poverty, so we have no loop. In row 1, column 3, we see that poverty causes disease, and in row three, column 1, we see that disease causes poverty. Both signs are the same (positive), so we have identified a deviation-amplifying loop: the poorer you are, the sicker you get, and the sicker you are, the poorer you get.

A person could go through the whole matrix this way, listing all of the loops, but matrix mathematics provide a quicker method. If we simply multiply the causal element map by its transpose, the resulting matrix will show us all of the loops and tell us whether they are deviation-amplifying or -limiting. (A companion disk available from the author will do the calculations for you.) This simply means laying rows on columns and multiplying them.

Row 1	0111	Row 2	0010	
Column 1	× 0011	Column 2	× 1000	etc.
	0011		0000	

The product becomes the new row and column of what we call a one-step loop table, which shows us where loops are and where they intersect. The completed matrix looks like Table 7.5.

To find an explosive cluster, look for a column (or row; they are identical in this matrix) that contains more than one positive value. Negative values indicate deviation-amplifying loops, which do not have the same explosive potential. This matrix shows us that poverty, disease, and drug abuse are all interconnected by mutually reinforcing loops—a disaster waiting to happen. The matrix also suggests that overcrowding is not tied into the cluster. It suggests, therefore (correctly so, I would editorialize) that jobs, health care, and drug-control should take priority over housing programs.

The loop table above contains no deviation-limiting loops. That is one reason the system it describes is so dangerous. The Eastern Title one-step loop table—more complex and fortunately more common—is shown in Table 7.6.

We find two clusters, one around volume and one around morale. The volume cluster is a headache for management but it is not explosive. Looking at the interrelationships, increased volume reduces speed, accuracy, availability of expertise, and client contacts, which in turn reduce volume. In order to keep these variables from constantly waxing and waning, management must balance trade-offs very carefully.

Table 7.5 One-Step Loop Table for Poverty, Overcrowding, Disease, and Drug Abuse

	1	2	3	4
1. Poverty	0	0	1	1
2. Overcrowding	0	0	0	0
3. Disease	1	0	0	0
4. Drug Abuse	1	0	0	0

Table 7.6 Eastern Title One-Step Loop Table

	1	2	3	4	5	6	7	8	9	10
1. Volume	0	-1	-1	0	0	-1	0	1	0	-1
2. Speed	-1	0	1	0	0	0	0	0	0	0
3. Accuracy	-1	1	0	0	0	0	0	0	1	0
4. C. Sat.	0	0	0	0	0	0	0	0	1	0
5. Losses	0	0	0	1	0	0	0	0	1	0
6. Expertise	-1	0	0	0	0	0	0	0	0	0
7. Resolve	0	0	0	0	0	0	0	0	1	0
8. Prioritize	1	0	0	0	0	0	0	0	0	0
9. Morale	0	0	1	1	1	0	1	0	0	0
10. Contacts	-1	0	0	0	0	0	0	0	0	0
Sums	5	2	3	2	1	1	1	1	4	1

Up to the time of the case study, this had not been the practice. Rather, evaluations and reward practices had focused on volume without recognizing that other variables have to be maintained to sustain desired volume levels. This led to role conflict, as employees struggled with conflicting demands not explicitly recognized by the organization.

The volume cluster is important and challenging, but the really interesting cluster, from both a positive and a negative standpoint, is the morale cluster. Rather than one variable straining against and ultimately correcting the excesses of the other, as is the case with the deviation-limiting loops of the volume cluster, the variables in the morale cluster multiply each other for good or ill.

Decreases in morale can lead to decreases in accuracy, in customer satisfaction, and inability to resolve customer problems, and to increases in losses, all of which further decrease morale. Left to itself, this chain of events can destroy the organization. If management is aware of this process and takes steps to identify thresholds at which such clusters become activated, proper monitoring and remedial action can avert disaster.

On the bright side, increases in one variable can lead to improvement in others, and the cycle can become more intensive over time, leading to a strong competitive advantage that other competitors will have to struggle to replicate.

More could be said about loops. We have only dealt with one-step loops, while others have developed more complex schemes. (If you really want to go crazy, see Bugon et al. 1977 and Voyer and Faulkner 1986). For most managers and consultants, though, the above description should tell you all you really need to know about loops. I will now show how cause maps and network concepts can be very profitably combined.

Cause Maps and the Activity System

Not only is cause mapping useful for troubleshooting specific operational problems and detecting dangerous situations, it can be extended to evaluate the general structure of the entire organization. In the Nelson and Mathews (1991a) article, there is a sophisticated and technically daunting way to do this, but the procedure below is much simpler and will provide many of the same insights.

All you do is juxtapose the formal departments or even individual positions with the variables from the cause map in a new matrix called (not surprisingly) a juxtaposition matrix. Although the order is arbitrary, it is easiest to place departments or positions in the rows and causal variables in columns. Then, working row by row, place a 1 in those columns for which the department has some responsibility or influence.

In the Eastern Title case, data processing, which we will place in row 1, has an impact on accuracy and losses (variables 3 and 5). Accounting (row 4) is identical to data processing. Policy (row 3) influences speed and losses. Like the cause map, the juxtaposition matrix can be completed by top management, a staff person, by everyone concerned, or in a group setting. The particular method depends on the degree of participation and consensus desired. Completing all of the rows we get the matrix shown in Table 7.7.

Like the row and column sums of the cause map, summary statistics from the juxtaposition matrix can yield useful information. The overall sum of the matrix tells us to what degree responsibility for important outcomes is dispersed throughout the organization. Maximum possible dispersion would consist of 1's in all cells for a total of 90 and would be expressed as a density of one computed in the same way that densities are computed for sociomatrices. This would suggest either a highly decentralized organization or one in which the activity system makes minimal use of the benefits of a rational division of labor.

Table 7.7 Eastern Title Juxtaposition Matrix (Simplified Version)

Departments	Variables										
	1	*2*	*3*	*4*	*5*	*6*	*7*	*8*	*9*	*10*	*Sums*
1. Data Processing	0	0	1	0	1	0	0	0	0	0	2
2. Exam	0	1	1	0	1	1	0	1	1	0	6
3. Policy	0	1	0	0	1	0	0	0	0	0	2
4. Accounting	0	0	1	0	1	0	0	0	0	0	2
5. Residential Closing	1	1	1	1	1	1	1	1	0	1	9
6. Marketing	1	0	0	0	0	0	0	0	0	1	2
7. Commercial Closing	1	1	1	1	1	1	1	1	1	1	10
8. Branch Closing	1	1	1	1	1	0	1	1	0	1	8
9. Runners	0	1	0	1	0	0	0	0	0	1	3
Sums	4	6	6	4	7	3	3	4	2	5	44

Variables:
  1. Volume
  2. Speed
  3. Accuracy
  4. Customer Satisfaction
  5. Losses
  6. Availability of Expertise
  7. Resolve Client Concerns
  8. Prioritize Searches
  9. Morale
10. Contacts

The Ideal Activity System

In an ideal activity system, each unit or position would be responsible for only one or two variables. As a rule, any reorganization should attempt to reduce the total density of the juxtaposition matrix, as this greatly simplifies workflow and coordination needs in the organization. Very low juxtaposition matrix densities indicate a very well-structured activity system, a very simple business, or both. This is seldom possible because of the complexities inherent in most businesses. It is particularly elusive in the title business and other organizations where services are delivered in a finite period and restricted space. It is, however, a worthy orienting principle.

The column sums indicate the degree to which responsibility for a given variable is diffused across the organization. The greater this diffusion, the more vigilant top management will have to be to see that the factor is handled adequately, and the more people will have to be involved in the project. The more departmentally contained a variable is, the more the factor can be delegated. For example, the ability to resolve client concerns and the availability of technical expertise are largely the concern of the closing departments; hence these issues can be dealt with on a departmental basis. On the other hand, speed, accuracy, and losses are influenced by 6, 6, and 7 units, respectively, requiring lots of contact and coordination to obtain a desirable result. Losses especially must be carefully watched by top management because they are influenced by many departments and influence the financial health of the company directly.

The row sums indicate the number of different variables for which a given department is responsible. This indicates the centrality of the unit to the mission of the organization and is a good indicator of the degree of complexity involved in managing the unit. Not surprisingly, the closing units are highest in row sums. The support departments, data processing, accounting, and runners, are lowest. We would accordingly expect the management of the former to be much more complex and require more frequent internal contact.

These departments are no place to start a management trainee. Instead they should start in the simpler units and work their way up. For example, at Eastern Title, an ideal trajectory is for an employee to begin in data processing with record transcription, then to move to examination, then perhaps to closing, then back to examination as a manager, and finally to closing as a manager. Thus, from a department with responsibility for two variables one would move to one with responsibility for four, and so on.

However informative the row and column sums, the juxtaposition matrix proper contains much more detailed information that can orient specific concerns. For instance, from the body of the juxtaposition matrix we can surmise that a task force on developing technical expertise would need to include members from examination, residential closing, and commercial closing (see column 6). It is also clear that commercial closing has its finger in a lot of pies—or rather, all of them. This gives one pause to think about whether the location of all three senior executives in commercial closing is the best policy.

If downsizing is going to force a merging of departments, or if increased size is going to demand the insertion of another layer of management, the juxtaposition matrix provides suggestions about how this may be done. The fact that the row vectors of both accounting and data processing are identical (i.e., they deal with the same variables) makes them prime candidates for consolidation or assignment to a span-breaking manager. To find compatible departments or functions, a person could compare every row vector to every other for similarities or simply run CONCOR on the transpose of the the juxtaposition matrix to discover what natural groupings exist.

The Furniture Factory

Like sociometric or CVAT data, the more cause maps you have inspected, the more meaningful the information from a given map will be. Another interesting cause map comes from a colleague of mine who has spent most of his working life in a family-owned wood furniture factory. The plant employs about fifty people and has been in business for over fifty years. My colleague identified the following variables as critical to the wood furniture business:

1. Skill level of workers
2. Quality of finished product
3. Inventory, both in process and finished product
4. Volume of orders
5. Competence of management
6. Attendance
7. Organization of workflow
8. Skill of sales staff
9. Strategic vision
10. Resistance to change

Notice that this list is much broader ranging than the Eastern Title variable list, which was much more focused on operational concerns. In this case, many of the differences in the list stem from the fact that the title business is highly legalistic and constrained by regulations, price controls, and geographical boundaries, while the wood furniture business is much more fluid, price sensitive, and susceptible to all kinds of product differentiation.

On the other hand, the complexion of the two maps is also a matter of the attentional focus and thinking of the employees of the title company versus the factory manager, and such differences in variable lists can be an indication of deficiencies in an organization or of an individual's vision. Particularly if you have occasion to work with more than one organization in the same business, a comparison of cause maps can reveal a lot about strengths, weaknesses, and blind spots in the respective companies' thinking. Similar observations can be made with individual maps, but that is another book.

Keeping these considerations in mind, lets look at the cause map to the furniture, displayed in Table 7.8.

Although the variables are somewhat different from those of the title company, the overall density of the matrix is almost identical (43/90 for the furniture factory versus 45/90 for the title company). Inventory and resistance to change appear to be major variables in this person's mind. According to my source "inventory covereth a multitude of sins," but it also "leadeth into temptation." In other words, a large cushion of inventory can compensate

Table 7.8   Furniture Plant Cause Map

	1	2	3	4	5	6	7	8	9	10	Sums
1. Worker Skills	0	1	1	0	1	1	1	0	0	−1	6
2. Quality	0	0	0	1	0	0	0	0	0	0	1
3. Inventory	0	1	0	1	−1	−1	−1	0	−1	−1	7
4. Order Volume	0	−1	−1	0	1	0	−1	0	0	0	4
5. Man. Competence	0	1	−1	0	0	1	1	0	1	−1	6
6. Attendance	0	1	0	0	1	0	1	0	0	0	3
7. Workflow Org.	1	1	0	0	0	0	0	0	0	1	3
8. Sales Skill	0	0	−1	1	0	0	0	0	0	0	2
9. Strat. Vision	0	1	−1	1	0	0	1	0	0	0	4
10. Resist. Change	−1	−1	1	−1	−1	0	−1	0	−1	0	7
Sums (Absolute)	2	8	6	5	5	3	7	0	3	4	43

for many managerial slipups, product defects, and scheduling deficiencies, but it also encourages laxity in a number of areas. Resistance to change is seen as the other villain here, probably because of the static, craft nature of furniture building and the family nature of the business.

The net influence index is similar to that of the title company except that the furniture business features less extreme values generally, suggesting that there may be fewer opportunities for leveraging change by working with just one or two major variables (see Table 7.9).

The one-step loop table is again similar but exhibits fewer intersecting loops (see Table 7.10).

Although both maps have the same number of loops, the title company has one variable (volume) in which five loops intersect, and one variable (morale) which hosts four deviation-amplifying loops. For the furniture factory, the loops are more dispersed, with only three amplifying loops on one variable and one variable with four loops of mixed types. This suggests that while the furniture business cannot be as easily leveraged from single variables, it is slightly less tricky in the sense that it has less explosive potential and less balancing of complex trade-offs.

The Cycle Shop

One last case illustrates further both how cause maps vary and what common features they tend to share. (I am indebted to Jim Jarvis of Cycle Tech, Carbondale, Illinois, for his contribution to this section.) This map comes from the owner of a motorcycle repair shop that also sells accessories and used bikes. It holds no dealer franchises and has been under the current

Table 7.9   Furniture Plant Net Influence Index

Variables	1	2	3	4	5	6	7	8	9	10
Outdegree	6	1	7	4	6	3	3	2	4	7
Indegree	–(2	8	6	5	5	3	7	0	3	4)
Net Influence Index	4	–7	1	–1	1	0	–4	2	1	3

Table 7.10   Furniture Plant Loop Table

	1	2	3	4	5	6	7	8	9	10
1. Worker Skills	0	0	0	0	0	0	1	0	0	1
2. Quality	0	0	0	–1	0	0	0	0	0	0
3. Inventory	0	0	0	–1	1	0	0	0	1	–1
4. Order Volume	0	–1	–1	0	0	0	0	0	0	0
5. Man. Competence	0	1	1	0	0	1	0	0	0	1
6. Attendance	0	0	0	0	1	0	0	0	0	0
7. Workflow Org.	1	0	0	0	0	0	0	0	0	–1
8. Sales Skill	0	0	0	0	0	0	0	0	0	0
9. Strat. Vision	0	1	1	0	0	0	0	0	0	0
10. Resist. Change	1	–1	–1	0	1	0	–1	0	0	0
Sums (Absolute)	2	1	4	2	3	1	2	0	1	3

management for about eight years. The owner identified the following ten variables as most important to his business:

1. Reputation
2. Price
3. Friendliness
4. Inventory
5. Honesty
6. Knowledgeable personnel
7. Reliability
8. Cash flow
9. Quality of work
10. Product selection

The list is self-explanatory except perhaps for reliability, which refers to having work done when promised and keeping predictable hours. Note how this list is less abstract than the furniture factory list and simpler in its concepts than the title company list. The list is also more customer-oriented than the other two lists—reputation, friendliness, honesty, and reliability all speak directly to customer concerns. This is both a reflection of the particular firm, which is highly customer-oriented, and the retail nature of the business. (Note again how cause maps provide insights into businesses and their cultures.) The repair of motorcycles per se obviously requires technical ability, but this ability is largely administered by individual mechanics working in occasional consultation with other staff. The real essence of the business, at least in the owner's mind, is understanding and satisfying customer needs while making money.

The cycle shop's cause map is shown in Table 7.11.

In several ways, this cause map suggests that the cycle business is simpler than either the title or furniture businesses. The density is considerably lower: 32/39 versus 45/90 and 43/90. This means that there is simply less going on than in the other two businesses. Moreover, looking at the indegrees (column sums) we see that three variables, Reputation, Price, and Knowledgeable Personnel account for 25 out of 32 causal links in the matrix. The upside of this is that, if you have these three variables under control, there is little else you have to worry about.

On the downside, there is little available in the way of variables that can leverage the whole system. In the title business, availability of expertise influences six other variables. In the furniture business, worker skills and resistance to change together affect seven other variables. In the cycle business, knowledgeable personnel leverages four other variables, but otherwise influence is either dispersed or negative (see Table 7.12).

The one step loop table further reinforces the comparative simplicity of the cycle business (see Table 7.13).

Instead of ten loops like the other two businesses, the cycle shop has only six (twelve divided by two), and four variables contain no loops at all. Of the six loops, only one is deviation-limiting. While a preponderance of deviation-amplifying loops means that things can get out of hand if not watched, the dearth of deviation-limiting loops means that the painstaking calculation and monitoring of optimal trade-offs is not as characteristic of this business as it is of, say, the title company.

The amplifying loops do combine to create two sensitive spots, though. Cash flow, quality, and product selection form a potential explosive cluster with price at the same time that price and reputation interact. This creates a tricky situation where the shop has a favorable reputation for low prices, but low prices can damage quality, cash flow, and selection, which can loop around and damage prices further.

There is also a dangerous situation around cash flow which can limit or enhance product selection, knowledgeable personnel, and prices. Unlike the title and furniture business, the cycle shop has a somewhat simpler world but one in which a few key variables must be watched very carefully.

Table 7.11 Cycle Shop's Cause Map

	1	2	3	4	5	6	7	8	9	10	Sums
1. Reputation	0	1	0	0	0	0	0	1	0	0	2
2. Price	-1	0	0	0	0	0	0	1	1	1	4
3. Friendliness	1	0	0	0	0	0	0	1	0	0	2
4. Inventory	1	-1	0	0	0	0	1	0	0	0	3
5. Honesty	1	0	0	0	0	0	0	1	0	0	2
6. Knowl. Per.	1	1	0	0	0	0	1	1	1	0	5
7. Reliability	1	1	0	0	0	0	0	1	0	0	3
8. Cash Flow	0	1	0	1	0	1	0	0	0	1	4
9. Work Quality	1	1	0	0	0	0	1	1	0	0	4
10. Product Sel.	1	1	0	0	0	0	0	1	0	0	3
Sums (Absolute)	8	7	0	1	0	1	3	8	2	2	32

Table 7.12 Cycle Shop's Net Influence Index

Variables	1	2	3	4	5	6	7	8	9	10
Outdegree	2	4	2	3	2	5	3	4	4	3
Indegree	-(8	7	0	1	0	1	3	8	2	2)
Net Influence Index	-6	-3	2	2	2	4	0	-4	2	1

Table 7.13 Cycle Shop's Loop Table

	1	2	3	4	5	6	7	8	9	10
1. Reputation	0	-1	0	0	0	0	0	0	0	0
2. Price	-1	0	0	0	0	0	0	1	1	1
3. Friendliness	0	0	0	0	0	0	0	0	0	0
4. Inventory	0	0	0	0	0	0	0	0	0	0
5. Honesty	0	0	0	0	0	0	0	0	0	0
6. Knowl. Per.	0	0	0	0	0	0	0	1	0	0
7. Reliability	0	0	0	0	0	0	0	0	0	0
8. Cash Flow	0	1	0	0	0	1	0	0	0	1
9. Work Quality	0	1	0	0	0	0	0	0	0	0
10. Product Sel.	0	1	0	0	0	0	0	1	0	0
Sums (Absolute)	1	4	0	0	0	1	0	3	1	2

Things to Look for in All Maps

Although our three maps differed in variables used, density of the resulting matrices, and the number and types of loops, our cases point up some common features and concerns that seem to be found in most businesses. The net influence index suggests that all variables are not created equal. Upon examining the indegrees and outdegrees of many maps Bugon et al. (1977) suggested three distinct types of cause map variables—givens, means, and ends.

Givens, Means, and Ends

Givens are variables that impact many other variables, but are themselves influenced by few. They are identified by a large positive value on the net influence index. If, like the weather, a given is difficult to manipulate, it must be worked around. However, many givens are ideal levers for change, as we observed earlier. In all three of our cases, worker skills or technical expertise were givens.

Ends are the opposite of givens in the sense that they come at the end of the causal chain. These are variables that are caused by a number of other variables but that impact few. Their net influence index is negative. Ends are important because they are usually outputs of the activity system and are central to organizational performance. Typical ends are quality, sales volume, scrap rates, losses, and customer satisfaction measures.

Ends are important measures of organizational health and should be watched closely, but they are seldom influenced directly. Usually they are managed by manipulating means, which come between givens and ends. Means have net influence values of 0 to positive 2 or 3. If one has strong, manipulable givens, one can concentrate efforts there and the means will sometimes take care of themselves. Most of the time, however, means have to be actively managed, and sometimes they present trade-offs. A good general maxim for the three variable types is: Watch the ends, leverage the givens, and manage the means.

Judging Ease of Management

Cause maps can be useful in predicting how hard a business will be to run, and a good map should be obtained from an expert before making an acquisition or starting a business. Unless you have considerable industry experience, look for acquisitions that have one or two strong givens and three or fewer ends. You will probably have better luck in businesses with cause maps that contain a variable list similar to the businesses you know. Also, have extra capital prepared if you find clusters of deviation-amplifying loops in your map—until you master the trade-offs involved, you will need some slack to absorb errors and downturns.

A company with some potential explosive clusters can be a good acquisition if it is doing well. Positive loops tend to feed on themselves and create a sustainable competitive advantage. Fewer competitors will be around because they tend to blow themselves to smithereens. It is essential, though, that you keep the current management in at least an advisory role, as they will know what danger signs to watch for. No managerial tool can predict all of the problems and opportunities that can arise from the complex interrelations that occur between the many factors that influence a business. However, judicious use of cause mapping can greatly reduce the likelihood that foreseeable problems are missed. Like network analysis, it is well worth the minimal effort to learn and practice basic cause mapping.

Epilogue: A Parting Panacea

In a way, this book is a protest against two excesses. On the one hand, I wanted to write a book that rebels at the excessive complexity and irrelevance of much academic research by making accessible and relevant some of the academic work I most admire. On the other hand, I wanted to protest against the superficiality and oversimplification of much of the popular management literature by writing a book that proposes concrete, technically advanced methods for figuring out what is going on as opposed to amorphous, nontechnical panaceas that disregard disciplined diagnosis. For this reason, and because of the nature of the material covered, I have refrained from touting my methods as unique, empowering, revolutionary, divinely approved, or otherwise capable of solving all of your problems.

However, now that I'm almost done and I've behaved myself for more than fifty-thousand words, I feel I am entitled to a short hypocritical benediction containing some glitzy, cure-all principles that will solve all of your problems and bring you happiness and wealth. So in closing, I want to share with you a few generalizations about how to avoid the many dysfunctions, problems, and pitfalls that this book has supposedly taught you to uncover. Although these principles are not directly derivable from the concepts or methods in this book, I think that they are expressive of the kind of mindset you need to diagnose and fix organizations.

Principle 1: Cultivate disciplined inquiry and critical reflection.

A prerequisite to profitably using the ideas and techniques in this book is the disposition to step back for a moment and look long and hard at large pieces of the organization. No question about it, this takes some time and money (although this book has focused on methods than can be carried out with fairly little external expense). The bigger hurdle, however, is the tendency to avoid self-examination. I believe that any organization that is to survive over time must develop the disposition and ability to seek out its weaknesses.

Principle 2: Practice foresight.

A common flaw in ill-fated decisions is a lack of "what ifs?" uttered at critical times. I know it is important not to kill initiative, and I know that people need to have room to make mistakes (especially small ones). But it seems to me that organizations tend to use their critical faculties differentially. If it is in style, or if the boss wants it, discussion is mercifully short. If not, discussion is bludgeoned to death. Any big decision needs to face the same evenhanded treatment, and a major part of this treatment should be the generation of alternative scenarios and evaluation of their consequences.

Although my only reference to the military in this book was the hostage mission fiasco, military special operations are among the best examples of how to practice foresight. Far from being the impulsive, snake-eating, Ramboesque maniacs portrayed by the media, special operations people are masters of foresight. They will not even consider a plan that has not been thought out hundreds of times in every detail, with multiple contingency plans and tireless rehearsals. And because of this, they seldom fail.

Principle 3: Develop constructive confrontation.

People and organizations tend to fall into two categories: either they pounce at the slightest provocation, or they bottle up disagreements until there is a major explosion. One of the advantages of a dispassionate, disciplined, if plodding, diagnosis is that it favors neither extreme. Organizations that survive over time develop ways of handling dissent and displeasure that avoid creating scars but also succeed in fully airing issues.

This is a big topic about which much has been written and more needs to be written. Look into the literature and become acquainted with good grievance- and conflict-management techniques. If you already have a history of serious conflict, developing constructive confrontation will require the services of a third party. This is money well spent.

Principle 4: There's no substitute for integrity.

Over the long term, people and organizations without integrity should and will fail. I hope you and your organization have integrity, and I hope you don't fail. In this country, business organizations (particularly the smaller ones) are the main engines of economic growth and innovation. We need you.

Appendix

Culture Matrix and Scoring Sheet

Culture Matrix

	Have Your Way	Status	Political (Wheeler-Dealer)	Leadership	Theory/ Analysis	Organization/ Details	Exposition/ Presentation	Flexibility/ Risk Taking	Total
Hard Work									
Time									
Finish Job									
Quality									
Warmth									
Empathy									
Sociability									
Loyalty									
Total									

Instructions: For each box in the matrix, draw a horizontal or vertical arrow to indicate which of the two values are more important to the organization or individual being studied. Sum horizontal arrows across rows and vertical arrows down columns to compute totals.

Graph for Culture Matrix

Work

    A Effort

    B Time

    C Finish Job

    D Quality

Relations

    E Affect

    F Empathy

    G Sociability

    H Loyalty

Control

    I   Dominance

    J   Status

    K Political

    L Leader

Thought

    M Abstract

    N Plan Organization

    O Exposition

    P Flexibility

0   1   2   3   4   5   6   7   8

References and Related Bibliography

Alderfer, Clayton L. 1969. An empirical test of a new theory of human needs. *Organizational Behavior and Human Performance,* May: 142–175.

Aldrich, Howard E. 1978. *Organizations and environments.* Englewood Cliffs, NJ: Prentice-Hall.

Ambrugey, Terry L., Dawn Kelly, and William P. Barnett. 1993. Resetting the clock: The dynamics of organizational change and failure. *Administrative Science Quarterly,* 38: 51–73.

Argenti, John. 1976. *Corporate collapse: The causes and symptoms.* Maidenhead, UK: McGraw-Hill.

Argyris, Chris. 1964. *Integrating the individual and the organization.* New York: Wiley.

Axlerod, R. 1976. *The structure of decision.* Princeton, NJ: Princeton University Press.

Barley, Stephen R., Gordon W. Meyer, and Debbie C. Gash. 1988. The culture of cultures: Academics, practitioners and the pragmatics of normative control. *Administrative Science Quarterly,* 31: 24–60.

Barnes, J. H., Jr. 1984. Cognitive biases and their impact on strategic planning. *Strategic Management Journal,* 5: 129–137.

Bennis, Warren. 1966. *Changing organizations.* New York: McGraw-Hill.

Binzen, Peter, and Joseph R. Daughen. 1971. *The wreck of the Penn Central.* Boston: Little, Brown.

Blake, Robert R., and Jane W. Mouton, 1964. *The managerial grid.* Houston: Gulf.

Blau, Peter M., and Richard M. Scott. *Formal organizations: A comparative approach.* San Francisco: Chandler Publishing Co., 1962.

Bossevain, Jeremy. 1974. *Friends of friends: Networks, manipulators, and coalitions.* Oxford: Basil-Blackwell.

Bozeman, B., and E. A. Slusher. 1979. Scarcity and environmental stress in public organizations: A conjectural essay. *Administration and Society,* 11: 335–356.

Breiger, Ronald L., S. A. Boorman, and Phipps Arabie. 1975. An algorithm for clustering relational data, with applications to social network analysis and comparison with multidimensional scaling. *Journal of Mathematical Psychology,* 12: 328–383.

Brieger, Ronald L., and Phillipa E. Pattison. 1978. The joint role structure of two community elites. *Sociological Methods and Research,* 7: 213–226.

Bugon, M., K. Weick, and D. Binkhorst. 1977. Cognition inorganizations: An analysis of the Utrecht jazz orchestra. *Administrative Science Quarterly,* 2: 606–639.

Cameron, Kim S. 1980. Critical questions in assessing organizational effectiveness. *Organizational Dynamics,* 9 (Autumn): 66–80.

Cameron, Kim S., David M. Whetton, and M. U. Kim. 1987. Organizational dysfunctions of decline. *Academy of Management Journal, 30*: 126–138.

Cavan, Sheri. 1966. *Liquor license: An ethnography of bar behavior.* Chicago: Aldine.

Chandler, Alfred, 1977. *The visible hand: The managerial revolution in American capitalism.* Cambridge, MA: Harvard Belknap Press.

Dahrendorf, Ralf. 1959. *Class and class conflict in industrial society.* Stanford, CA: Stanford University Press.

Da Mata, Roberto. 1978. *Carnavais, malandros e herois.* Rio: Zahar.

D'Aveni, R. A. 1989. Dependability, the organizational bankruptcy: An application of agency and prospect theory. *Management Science, 35*: 1120–1138.

Davis, Tim R. 1984. The Influence of physical environment in office. *Academy of Management Review, 9*: 271–283.

Dittenfass, Michael. 1988. Entrepreneurial failure reconsidered: The case of the interwar British coal industry. *Business History Review, 62*: 1–35.

French, John R., and Bertram Raven. 1962. The bases of social power. In Dorwin Cartwright, ed., *Group dynamics: Research and theory,* pp. 607–623. Evanston, IL: Row Peterson.

Gillin, John. 1952. *Moche: A Peruvian coastal community.* Institute of Social Anthropology, Publication 3. Washington, DC: Smithsonian Institution.

Glaser, Barney G., and Anselm L. Strauss. 1967. *The discovery of grounded theory.* Chicago: Aldine.

Good, Bill. 1981 *Prospecting your way to sales success.* New York: Scribners.

Gopalan, Suresh. 1991. An emirpical investigation of the relationship between organizational and national cultures in the United States, India, and Brazil. Ph.D. dissertation, Louisiana Tech University.

Gopalan, Suresh, John Dittrich, and Reed E. Nelson. 1994. Analysis of organization culture: A critical stop in mergers and acquisitions. *Journal of Business Strategies, 11*: 124–140.

Gordon, Robert, and James Howell. 1959. *Modern education for business.* New York: Columbia University Press.

Granovetter, Mark. 1973. The strength of weak ties. *American Journal of Sociology, 78*: 1360–1380.

Greenhalgh, L. Maintaining organizational effectiveness during organizational retrenchment. *Journal of Applied Behavioral Science, 18* (1982): 155–170.

Hadley, Arthur Twinning. 1986. *The straw giant: Triumph and failure in America's armed forces: A report from the field.* New York: Random House.

Hall, Richard H. 1976. *Organizations: Structure, process, and outcomes.* Englewood Cliffs, NJ: Prentice-Hall.

Hall, Richard H. 1991. *Organizations: Structures, processes, and outcomes.* 5th ed. Englewood Cliffs, NJ: Prentice-Hall.

Hambrick, D. C., and R. A. D'Aveni. 1988. Large corporate failures as downward spirals. *Administrative Science Quarterly, 33*: 1–23.

Hannan, M. T., and J. Freeman. 1984. Structural inertia and organizational change. *American Sociological Review, 49*: 149–164.

Hartley, Robert F. 1986. *Management mistakes,* 2d ed. New York: Wiley.

Hawken, Paul. 1987. *Growing a business.* New York: Fireside Books.

Hawkins, John. 1984. *Inverse images: The meaning of culture, ethnicity, and family in postcolonial Guatemala*. Albuquerque: University of New Mexico Press.

Hodgetts, Richard M. 1988. *Management: Theory Process and Practice*. 4th ed. Orlando, FL: Dryden Press.

Homans, George A. 1950. *The human group*. New York: Harcourt Brace.

Janis, I. L. 1982. *Groupthink*. Boston: Houghton Mifflin.

Jerimer, John M. Slocum, Louis E. Fry, and Jeannie Gaines. 1991. Organizational subcultures in a soft bureaucracy: Resistance behind the myth and facade of an official culture. *Organization Science, 2*: 170–194.

Jick, Todd, and V. V. Murray. 1982. The management of hard times: Budget cutbacks in public sector organizations. *Organization Studies, 3*: 141–170.

Katz, D., and R. L. Kahn. 1978. *The social psychology of organizations,* 2d ed. New York: Wiley.

Keesing, Roger M. 1974. Theories of culture. *Annual Review of Anthropology, 3*: 73–97.

Kets de Vries, Manfred R., and Danny Miller. 1984. Neurotic style and organizational pathology. *Strategic Management Journal, 5*: 35–55.

Kets de Vries, Manfred R., and Danny Miller. 1984. *The neurotic organization*. San Francisco: Jossey-Bass.

Kets de Vries, Manfred R., et al. 1991. *Organizations on the couch: Clinical perspectives on organizational behavior and change*. San Francisco: Jossey-Bass.

Kimberly, J., and R. E. Miles. 1980. *The organizational life cycle*. San Francisco: Jossey-Bass.

Klein, J. I. 1988. The myth of the corporate political jungle: Politicization as a political strategy. *Journal of Management Studies*, January: 1–11.

Kotter, John, and J. Heskett. 1992. *Corporate culture and performance*. New York: Free Press.

Krackhardt, David M., and Martin Kilduff. 1990. Friendship patterns and culture: The control of organizational diversity. *American Anthropologist, 92*: 142–154.

Krackhardt, David, and Robert N. Stern. The structuring of informal organizations and the management of crises. *Social Psychology Quarterly, 51* (1988): 123–140.

Larson, Lars R., Jerry G. Hunt, and Richard H. Osborne. 1976. The great hi-hi leader behavior myth: A lesson from Occam's razor. *Academy of Management Journal*, December: 628–641.

Lauman, Edward O., and Franz Pappi. 1976. *Networks of collective action*. New York: Academic Press.

Lawrence, P. R. , and J. W. Lorsch. 1967. *Organization and environment*. Boston: Harvard University Press.

Levi Strauss, Claude. 1963. *Structural anthropology*. New York: Basic Books.

March, James G. 1991. Exploration and exploitation in organizational learning. *Organization Science, 2*: 71–87.

Mausch, Michael. 1985. Vicious circles in organizations. *Administrative Science Quarterly, 22*: 606–639.

McClelland, David C. 1961. *The achieving society*. Princeton, NJ: Von Nostrand Reinhold.

Merton, Robert K. 1957. *Social theory and social structure*. Glencoe, IL: Free Press.

Meyer, Marshall W., and Lynne G. Zucker. 1989. *Permanently failing organizations.* Newbury Park, CA: Sage.

Milburn, T. W., R. S. Schuler, and K. H. Watman. 1983. Organizational crisis—Part I: Definition and conceptualization; Part II: Strategies and responses. *Human Relations, 36* (12): 1141–1180.

Miles, Raymond E., and Charles C. Snow. 1978. *Organization strategy, structure and process.* New York: McGraw-Hill.

Miller, Danny. 1993. The architecture of simplicity. *Academy of Management Review, 18*: 116–138.

Mintzberg, Henry. 1979. *The structuring of organizations.* Englewood Cliffs, NJ: Prentice-Hall.

Mintzberg, Henry. 1983. *Power in and around organizations.* Englewood Cliffs, NJ: Prentice-Hall.

Misra, Sarah Koovor. 1993. What causes organizational crises: A model of crisis causation. Unpublished manuscript, Department of Management, University of Colorado at Denver.

Mitroff, I. I., T. C. Pauchant, M. Finney, and C. Pearson. 1989. Do some organizations cause their own crises? The cultural profile of crisis-prone vs. crisis-prepared organizations. *Industrial Crisis Quarterly, 3*: 269–283.

Nance, J. J. 1984. *Splash of colors: The self destruction of Braniff International.* New York: William Morrow.

Nelson, Reed E. 1988. Social network analysis as intervention tool. *Group Organizations Studies, 13*: 39–58.

Nelson, Reed E. 1989. The strength of strong ties: Social networks and intergroup conflict in organizations. *Academy of Management Journal, 32*: 377–401.

Nelson, Reed E. 1990. A network approach to upper level management. *Business Insights, 8*: 49–54.

Nelson, Reed E., and K. Michael Mathews. 1991a. The use of cause maps and social network analysis in organizational diagnosis. *Journal of Applied Behavioral Science, 27*: 379–397.

Nelson, Reed E., and K. Michael Mathews. 1991b. The social networks of high performing organizations. *Journal of Business Communication, 28*: 367–386.

Nottenburg, G., and G. B. Fedor. 1983. Scarcity in the environment: Organizational perceptions, interpretations, and responses. *Organization Studies, 4*: 317–337.

Nystrom, Paul C. 1978. Managers and the great hi-hi leader myth. *Academy of Management Journal*, June: 325–331.

Oldham, Greg R., and Nancy L. Notchford. 1983. Relations between office characteristics or employee reactions. *Administrative Science Quarterly, 28*: 542–556.

O'Reily, Charles A., III, Jennifer Chatman and David F. Caldwell. 1988. People and organizational culture: A profile comparison approach to assessing person-organization fit. *Academy of Management Journal, 34*: 487–516.

Organ, Dennis W., and Thomas Bateman. 1992. *Organizational behavior.* Plano, TX: BPI.

Ouchi, William. 1981. *Theory 2: How American business can meet the Japanese challenge.* Reading, MA: Addison-Wesley.

Pauchant, Thierry, and Ian I. Mitroff. 1992. *Transforming the crisis prone organization.* San Francisco: Jossey-Bass.

Perrow, Charles. 1971. *Organizational analysis: A sociological view.* Belmont, CA: Brooks and Cole.

Perrow, C. 1984. *Normal accidents: Living with high risk technologies.* New York: Basic Books.

Peters, Thomas J., and R. H. Waterman. 1982. *In search of excellence.* New York: Harper and Row.

Pierson, Frank. 1959. *The education of American business.* New York: McGraw-Hill.

Radcliffe-Brown, Alfred R. 1952. *Structure and function in primitive society.* New York: Free Press.

Rousseau, Denise. 1990. Assessing organizational culture: The case for multiple methods. In Benjamin Schneider, ed., *Organizational climate and culture*, pp. 153–192. San Francisco: Jossey-Bass.

Saussure, Ferdinand de. 1959. *Course in general linguistics.* New York: McGraw-Hill.

Schon, Donald A. 1983. *The reflective practitioner: How professionals think in action.* New York: Basic Books.

Seiler, J. A. 1963. Diagnosing interdepartmental conflict. *Harvard Business Review, 41*: 121–132.

Selvin, Hanan C. 1951. The interplay of social research and social policy in housing. *Journal of Social Issues, 8*: 180–191.

Selznick, Philip. 1966. *TVA and the grass roots.* New York: Harper and Row.

Serling, R. J. 1980. *From the captain to the colonel: An informal history of Eastern Airlines.* New York: Dial Press.

Singer, Milton. 1968. Culture. *International encyclopedia of the social sciences, 3*: 527–543.

Stinchcombe, Arthur L. 1965. Social structure and organizations. In J. G. March, ed., *Handbook of organizations.* Chicago: Rand-Mcnally.

Straw, Barray M., L. E. Sandelands, and J. E. Dutton. 1981. Threat-rigidity effects in organizational behavior: A multilevel analysis. *Administrative Science Quarterly, 26*: 501–524.

Taylor, Fredrick W. 1911. *Principles of scientific management.* New York: Harper and Row.

Thompson, James D. 1967. *Organizations in action.* New York: McGraw Hill.

Tuchman, Barbara. 1984. *The march of folly.* New York: Knopf.

Turner, B. A. 1976. The organizational and interorganizational development of disasters. *Administrative Science Quarterly, 21*: 378–397.

Voyer, J. J., and R. R. Faulkner. 1986. Cognition and leadership in an artistic organization. In J. A. Pearce and R. B. Robinson, eds., *Academy of management best paper proceedings*, Chicago, pp. 160–164. Academy of Management.

Webb, E. J., D. T. Campbell, R. D. Schwarz, and L. Sechrest. 1966. *Unobtrusive measures: Non-reactive research in the social sciences.* Chicago: Rand-McNally.

Wegscheider, Sharon. 1981. *Another chance: Hope in health for the alcoholic family.* Palo Alto: Science and Behavior Books.

Weick, Karl. 1979. *The social psychology of organizing.* Reading, MA: Addison-Wesley.

Weick, Karl. 1987. Organizational culture as a source of high reliability. *California Management Review, 29*: 112–127.

Weitzel, William, and E. Johnson. 1989. Decline in organizations: A literature integration and extension. *Administrative Science Quarterly, 34*: 91–109.

Wheatly, Margaret J. 1992. *Leadership and the new science: Learning about organizations from an orderly universe.* San Francisco: Berrett Koehler.

Whetten, D. A. 1980. Sources, responses, and effects of organizational decline. In J. R. Kimberly and R. E. Miles, eds., *The organizational life cycle.* San Francisco: Jossey-Bass.

White, Harrison, S. Boorman, and Ronald L. Breiger. 1976. Social structure from multiple networks. 1. Blockmodels of roles and positions. *American Sociological Review, 20*: 661–668.

Wilkins, Alan L., and William G. Ouchi. 1983. Efficient cultures: Exploring the relationship between culture and organizational performance. *Administrative Science Quarterly, 28*: 468–481.

Woodward, Joan. 1965. *Industrial organization.* 4. Biographical sketch. London: Oxford University Press.

Index

About the Author

REED E. NELSON is an Associate Professor of Management at Southern Illinois University, with a doctorate in organizational behavior from Cornell. His research focuses on organizational dysfunctions and their diagnosis, and the role of culture in organizations. He is author of the widely used CVAT instruments and has published extensively in academic and professional business journals. He currently serves on the editorial board of *Administrative Science Quarterly*.